The Problem *of* PLURALISM

RECOVERING UNITED METHODIST IDENTITY

JERRY L. WALLS

Good News Books

WILMORE • KENTUCKY

The Problem of PLURALISM

Library of Congress Card Number: 86-82795
ISBN: 0-917-851-02-1
Suggested Subject Heading: Doctrine - United Methodist
Recommended Dewey Decimal Classification: 230.76

GOOD NEWS BOOKS
A division of Good News, A Forum for Scriptural Christianity, Inc.
308 East Main Street ● Wilmore, Kentucky 40390

To Patricia
Daughter of the
Wesleyan Tradition

Contents

ACKNOWLEDGEMENTS

Most of the material in Chapter Two of this book, and part of Chapter Three originally appeared in *Quarterly Review: A Scholarly Journal for Reflection on Ministry,* fall 1985, in an essay entitled "What is Theological Pluralism?" in a more condensed and edited form. This material is reprinted here with permission of The United Methodist Publishing House and the United Methodist Board of Higher Education and Ministry, copyright 1985. Chapter Four is an expanded version of a section from an essay entitled "Examining the Case for Pluralism" which originally appeared in *The Asbury Seminarian,* fall, 1983. Other portions of this essay are also incorporated into other chapters of this book. I am grateful to the editors of these journals for securing permission to reprint this material.

An earlier version of Chapter Five was read at the 1985 Christmas Conference of the John Wesley Fellows, in Shaker Village, Kentucky. The spirited discussion which followed led to a number of improvements. Thomas V. Morris and Laurence W. Wood also read and discussed this chapter with me and gave valuable advice.

A number of other persons read all or part of the manuscript and made helpful corrections and suggestions. These include: Robert G. Tuttle, Jr., Geoffrey Wainwright, James F. White, and John Wright. A special word of thanks must go to William J. Abraham, who wrote detailed and incisive comments on earlier versions of several chapters.

Thanks are due to Michael Sigler for his editorial work on the manuscript. Jurgen Braüer's efficient help in getting the manuscript on computer was appreciated. Thanks are also due to Tracy Balzer, who dealt cheerfully with the numerous revisions I sent her way. And a special word of appreciation goes to James V. Heidinger II and James S. Robb, whose enthusiasm for the project has been a source of great encouragement.

Finally, I wish to record my gratitude to my family. My wife Patricia provided warm support during the time spent on the book and also found time to type most of the first draft, despite her already demanding schedule. And although their contribution to this book is indirect at best, I must mention with affection my children Angela and Jonathan.

INTRODUCTION

The year 1984 was one of celebration for American Methodism. Two hundred years before, on December 24, 1784, Methodism had been officially organized as a distinct American church, at the famous "Christmas Conference" in Baltimore, Maryland. During 1984 the several branches of American Methodism united in a yearlong bicentennial commemoration.

1984 was also a time of serious reflection for American Methodism. Many were asking where Methodism had come after 200 years and which direction it would be headed as it entered its third century. Such questions were particularly evident in the largest branch of American Methodism, namely the United Methodist Church. Indeed, many observers felt that United Methodism had lost its direction. As Leonard I. Sweet, president of United Theological Seminary, graphically put it: "United Methodism ended its second century with all the clarity of vision of a wiperless windshield in the middle of a storm."[1]

The loss of direction in United Methodism can perhaps be seen most clearly by a brief look at the 1984 General Conference, held at Baltimore. A pre-conference survey of the delegates revealed that "most harbored deep concerns about a lack of unity within the United Methodist Church."[2] Without a sense of unity, there is no sense of common purpose or direction. Such lack of unity, moreover, undermines a church's sense of identity. For if United Methodists do not know what binds them together, they do not know who they are.

The delegates certainly had reason for concern in light of the number of divisive issues on the conference agenda. Some of these issues were highly controversial and received a good deal of noisy publicity. Foremost in terms of public controversy was the issue of homosexual ordination. Close behind was the well-publicized dispute over the World Council of Churches and National Council of Churches and the question of United Methodism's proper role in these organizations. Other emotional issues included abortion, a new independent Mission Society for United Methodists which had formed out of frustration with the policies of the denomination's official mission agency, and the report of a task force which recommended the use of sexually inclusive language in worship.

In the midst of all this controversy, however, conference delegates took action on some other matters which could have far more impact on the future of Methodism than any of the more publicized issues. These actions, while exposing the depth of United Methodism's problems with respect to direction and identity, also hold out the hope that direction can be found again and a sense of identity restored.

First, in the hope of gaining a renewed sense of direction, the conference called for a four-year study of the mission of the United Methodist Church. Those calling for the study frankly admitted that the church had lost its "unifying vision" and needed to recover such a vision in order to be effective.[3]

In a second significant action, conference delegates called for a commission to prepare a new Doctrinal Statement to be presented at the next General Conference in 1988. This action was particularly interesting because, just 12 years earlier, General Conference had adopted a new Doctrinal Statement which has been a part of the United Methodist *Discipline* since 1972. In calling for yet another new Statement, the 1984 conference clearly was expressing dissatisfaction with the 1972 Statement.

Why the need for another Doctrinal Statement so soon? One of the most frequently cited problems with the 1972 Statement was that it openly espoused "theological pluralism." That is to say, the Statement explicitly recognized as viable the whole range of viewpoints and options represented in contemporary theology. It has been widely felt that this open-ended attitude toward theology has projected confusion about what we believe as a church, and consequently, confusion about our very identity.[4]

Pluralism: Problem or Solution?

Of course, not all would agree that theological pluralism is a problem. Some view pluralism not as a drawback but an asset, not as a bane but a blessing.

This was certainly the case several years ago when pluralism was first adopted as official policy by the United Methodist Church. In 1972, the year pluralism was officially accepted, a book appeared which lauded pluralism in a way which reflects the spirit of the times. That book said doctrinal diversity "produces fruitful tension," that because we have taken the risk of affirming theological pluralism, "we may reap the rewards of a vital church, alive with ferment and dialogue," and that pluralism "constitutes not a threat but a promise."[5]

A decade ago, such heady statements may have struck a responsive note. Pluralism may then have seemed like the salvation of theology, if not the church. Pluralism freed us from the "Restrictive Rules"[6] which would bind us by formerly "established standards of doctrine." It could then be said with emphasis that Wesley's guidelines of Scripture, tradition, reason, and experience not only "allow for" but "positively encourage variety in United

Methodist theologizing" (*The Book of Discipline of the United Methodist Church,* p. 78. All *Discipline* quotes are from the 1984 edition, unless otherwise indicated). And did not this situation promise a bright future? As Bishop Colaw put it: "This [the acceptance of theological pluralism] can lead us to understand our faith in such a way that it will stimulate each of us to vital worship and celebration, significant evangelistic outreach, and meaningful social and missional application."[7]

Yet, how well has pluralism delivered its promises? Is the United Methodist Church stronger and more vital since theological pluralism was adopted as a guiding principle?

It is not my purpose here to debate the record of the United Methodist Church over the past decade. Nor is it my aim to try to document a correlation between statistics of institutional decline and theological pluralism. But I do want to ask: Has the affirmation of pluralism helped lay a solid theological foundation for ministry, or has the affirmation of pluralism contributed to the loss of a "unifying vision" for effective mission?

These surely are important questions if a sound and vital theology is essential for the effective ministry of the church. And on this point there is something of a consensus. As the *Discipline* puts it, there is:

> . . . general agreement that the United Methodist Church stands urgently in need of doctrinal reinvigoration for the sake of authentic renewal, fruitful evangelism, and the effective discharge of our ecumenical commitments. Seen in this light, the recovery and updating of our distinctive doctrinal heritage—"truly catholic, truly evangelical and truly reformed"—takes on a high priority (p. 50).

Has the official acceptance of theological pluralism led to the "recovery and updating" of the Wesleyan doctrinal heritage?

A growing body of evidence suggests otherwise, and that persons all across the United Methodist Church are having second thoughts about the validity of pluralism. The 1984 General Conference's call for a new Doctrinal Statement is most significant in this regard, but also worth noting are the slight changes that have already been made in the 1972 Statement, indicating unease with its affirmation of pluralism. For example, the 1972 Statement asserts that "pluralism should be recognized as a principle" (*Discipline,* 1972, p. 69). The 1980 *Discipline* tempers this somewhat by simply stating that "we recognize the presence of theological pluralism" (p. 72).

The former expression clearly affirms pluralism as a positive good. The latter, while ambiguous, could be taken merely as an empirical observation that the United Methodist Church exhibits considerable doctrinal diversity. And anyone would have to agree with that.

Then in 1984, this clause was revised yet again, to read: "we recognize under the guidance of our doctrinal standards and guidelines the presence of theological pluralism" (p. 72). This revision makes a rather halfhearted attempt to define some limits for pluralism, namely, our doctrinal standards.[8] Such changes, while moving in the right direction, are isolated, and the Doctrinal Statement as a whole still reflects a decidedly pluralistic perspective.

While concern over theological pluralism has become more widespread in recent times, opposition to the acceptance of pluralism was present from its inception, particularly among evangelicals and other traditionally inclined United Methodists. The evangelical organization Good News, for instance, has consistently addressed the problem of pluralism over the years. Indeed, Charles Keysor, the founder of Good News, predicted that the official acceptance of pluralism "will be recognized someday as the most serious mistake in the history of American Methodism."[9]

Why do evangelicals view the acceptance of theological pluralism as such a disaster? James V. Heidinger II, Keysor's successor as head of Good News, explains:

> Many evangelicals believe that a new era was inaugurated at the 1972 General Conference with the introduction of theological pluralism. The action may have been the abandonment of the historic Methodist doctrinal distinctives. That probably was not the intent of the Theological Study Commission, but evangelicals believe it has been the unfortunate result.[10]

Even more was at stake in the adoption of pluralism than historic Methodist distinctives, however. As Ira Gallaway charged in his prophetic book *Drifted Astray,* "The very term 'theological pluralism' is used to allow or condone almost any theological or ethical position—provided that position is within the psychological framework of a liberal and humanistic interpretation of faith and life."[11] In other words, the era of pluralism has witnessed far more than the loss of our distinctive Methodist doctrinal heritage. Even the most central doctrines of Christianity, which United Methodists share with others, must give way when appeal is made to "theological pluralism." Is it any wonder that United Methodists suffer an identity crisis, if the body of beliefs which formerly bound them together has crumbled under the impact of pluralism?

The charge that virtually any theological position is allowed within our church would, of course, be quickly denied by some. Bishop Jack M. Tuell, for instance, insists it is not true that "United Methodists can believe anything they want to." To substantiate his claim, Bishop Tuell cites the statement in our *Discipline* that: "There is a core of doctrine which informs in greater or lesser degree our widely divergent interpretations." Significantly, however, Bishop Tuell goes on to add:

> In recent years we have tended to lose sight of that central "core of doctrine" and have allowed ourselves as United Methodists to dwell on the "divergent interpretations," to which we have given the hideous name of "pluralism." And sometimes we have talked as though it is our "pluralism" which holds us together and which is our most distinctive mark! . . . To suggest this is to suggest only chaos and disintegration.[12]

It seems apparent, then, that the official acceptance of pluralism has generated deeper problems than it has solved. Instead of leading United Methodists to a greater understanding of their faith, it has caused them to lose sight of the core of doctrine which should bind them together. And this in turn has undermined the sort of unity which is needed for vital outreach and ministry.

The Forces of Transition

Before we plunge more deeply into the issues surrounding pluralism, it will be worthwhile to pause for a moment to consider briefly some of the developments which led to its ascendancy.

The acceptance of pluralism should be seen against the broad background of years of gradual theological transition. For Methodists did not move overnight from the adoption of the Restrictive Rules, which would establish traditional doctrinal standards, to the official acceptance of pluralism.[13] Broadly speaking, we can identify two currents of change which have done much to shape contemporary theology. First, there are historical factors; and second, there are intellectual movements.

On the historical side, we can begin by noting some of the political forces at work during the eighteenth-century Enlightenment, the period, significantly, during which Methodism was born. This was the age in which deism, a rationalistic religion which rejected special revelation, reached its height. The following quote sketches how this era made an impact on religious thinking.

> Perhaps the most widespread factor in the growth of Enlightenment religion was the mood of revulsion against the embattled creeds. Europe had been ravaged and brutalized by a century of religious warfare. . . . From the seventeenth into the nineteenth century the strongest argument for Enlightenment religion was the general experience that religious orthodoxy in power meant massacre, crusades, and persecution. . . . In place of persecution Enlightenment religion, with certain exceptions, stood for tolerance. On the negative side this implied a degree of scepticism or relativity with regard to rival theologies.[14]

An age which was weary of crusades for creeds naturally began to turn a critical eye toward the creeds themselves.

This climate of opinion surely had some impact on the formation of Methodism. These factors helped give shape to Wesley's own concept of "catholic spirit." He was far more concerned to promote holy living than any particular doctrine. He did not want Methodists to be identified by any distinctive confession of faith. This, no doubt, made it easier for Methodists to lose any sense of doctrinal cohesion. In a subsequent chapter we will consider whether Wesley's "catholic spirit" is a warrant for our church's stance on pluralism. But for now let us simply be clear on the point that Methodism was born in an atmosphere of growing toleration, and that this aspect of the Enlightenment left a permanent mark on Western thought and life.

Another historical point worth noting involves the early spread of Methodism on American soil. At this time, America was largely a frontier, and not well suited to all the regularities of organized religion. As the United

Methodist *Discipline* points out, American Christianity as a whole was transformed by the revivals of this period, with their increasing stress on "Christian experience." Among Methodists there was a corresponding decrease of emphasis on formal doctrinal standards. "By the end of the nineteenth century, and thereafter increasingly into the twentieth, Methodist theology had become decidedly eclectic, with less and less specific attention paid to its Wesleyan sources as such" (*Discipline*, p. 45). Developments such as these obviously help to explain the current diversity in United Methodist theology.

Closely related to these historical movements are some extremely important changes in the intellectual environment. These have to do primarily with new ideas in philosophy, science, and the nature of history. Many of these ideas were used to assault traditional Christian beliefs and doctrines.

We have already noted the rise of deism and its rejection of special revelation. The eighteenth century was also the age of Hume and Kant, who brought powerful arguments against traditional Christian views. Hume's attack on miracles, an essential element in the traditional account of divine revelation, is especially noteworthy. A number of other thinkers joined in casting doubt on our knowledge of the past, particularly the events recorded in Scripture. And Kant's critical work on the limits of human knowledge led many theologians to conclude we can have no real knowledge of God. These lines of thought, which radically challenge Christian belief, have extended into the twentieth century and still deeply influence much theological thinking.

Indeed, many of the most influential theologians of our age have rejected traditional understandings of revelation, including the miraculous. It has been widely held that traditional Christian beliefs are simply incompatible with modern canons of judgment, especially in science and history. This rejection by many of such basic elements of traditional Christianity resulted in the breakdown of even a general consensus in theology. In recent times this breakdown was demonstrated most vividly during the 1960s when a number of radical theological proposals gained notoriety, some of which even proclaimed the death of God. It was on the heels of this period, remember, that the 1972 Statement was adopted.

This brief sketch represents something of the broader context surrounding the United Methodist Church's official decision to sanction theological pluralism. I have included it to show that the problems which our church attempted to come to grips with in 1972 were, and are, real.

By way of summary, we may conclude that the following were major factors in the decision to officially accept pluralism: (1) There was a desire to avoid the unhealthy and unloving intolerance which has often attended efforts to maintain definite doctrinal standards. (2) A genuine effort was made to be faithful to the Wesleyan ideal of catholic spirit. (3) The pragmatic reality of the theological diversity which had grown up in Methodism over the decades had to be recognized. (4) The complete breakdown of consensus within the theological community at large discouraged any effort to define doctrine in normative terms.

Some Hard Questions

In this light it is at least understandable why our church, in its effort to come to honest terms with these difficulties, elected to make pluralism "a principle." Indeed, these difficulties were keenly felt by those who served on the Theological Commission on Doctrine and Doctrinal Standards, which recommended our present policy on pluralism. Bishop Emerson Colaw, who served on that commission reports:

It was felt that because of the tremendous variety of beliefs among United Methodists, we needed a new doctrinal statement. It was *quickly* decided that we could not develop a creed to which all in our church must give adherence. The commission even found it impossible to agree, for there were theologians and pastors and laymen who represented every sequence of the theological spectrum. We decided that doctrine could not be a legalistic nor juridical standard for excommunication or censure. All we could do was speak with assurance of emphases and directions which we hold in common and then let each board, each person, hammer out his own understanding of his faith and task.[15]

Here we see a group of official representatives of our church, whose theological views were so diverse that substantial agreement was impossible. Moreover, we clearly see a fear of intolerance, a fear that doctrinal standards may be improperly used. That the acceptance of theological pluralism was recommended by this commission should not be surprising.

While granting this, we may go on to ask a few hard questions. Is it not possible that the commission moved too "quickly" in its decision that a normative creed could not be developed for our church? Have we departed too hastily from the long tradition of the Church universal, which has always insisted that basic doctrine can and should be rather specifically defined?[16] Is it perhaps the case that we have become so fearful of narrow intolerance that we have lost our ability to draw any definite lines? Have we not been too willing to give ground to some of the intellectual movements against traditional Christianity? And is it not possible that some of the positions represented on the commission were not genuinely Christian? Why was this possibility not considered when it became apparent that substantial agreement could not be reached? Even among Christians who disagree sharply on secondary issues, should there not be profound agreement on basic doctrine?

Questions such as these, I think, are at the root of the growing unease in our church with theological pluralism. We should be willing to face them, even if it means admitting that a mistake was made in 1972. If pluralism was indeed accepted in an honest attempt to resolve real problems, our church should be equally honest in dealing with the difficulties in the present Doctrinal Statement, and the problems to which it has given rise.

Pluralism in Other Traditions

Thus far I have dealt with pluralism as it exists within the United Methodist Church. However, the problem of pluralism is not unique to United Methodism. The intellectual forces which underlie pluralism have been felt all across the Christian Church.

Consider the Roman Catholic Church, which is sometimes thought by outsiders to be monolithic in belief and practice. Recent years have seen increasingly vocal challenges to official doctrine as well as papal authority. Symbolic of this trend was an ad which appeared in the *New York Times* entitled "A Catholic Statement on Pluralism and Abortion." The ad, which was signed by 97 Roman Catholics, including three men who belong to religious orders, stated that "a diversity of opinion regarding abortion exists among committed Catholics."[17] To be sure, Pope John Paul II has sought to curb such dissidence, but the point remains that there is vast theological diversity within the Roman church.

Pluralism is also prevalent in the Anglican church. Indeed, the problem of pluralism is an important theme in the recent report of the Doctrine Commission of the Church of England entitled *Believing in the Church*. One of the authors of the report informs us that this question is often pressed by both outsiders and members of the Anglican church: "Are there *any* effective controls today over what ordained and licensed teachers of the church may say and write?"[18]

Other mainline Protestant denominations in America certainly have their share of difficulty with pluralism, too. This has been especially so since the resurgence of evangelicalism in the past decade or so. In his significant book, *Mainline Churches and the Evangelicals: A Challenging Crisis?*, Presbyterian Richard G. Hutcheson, Jr. shows clearly the practical problems which arise from pluralism.[19]

Even more conservative groups such as the Southern Baptists are not immune to the problems of pluralism. A struggle for control of the Southern Baptist Convention has been going on between conservatives and moderates for some time. The chief theological issue has been Biblical authority and the proper use of Biblical criticism.

What about the more conservative branches of the Wesleyan tradition? Is pluralism a problem with them also? A good barometer for measuring theological trends in these branches of the Church is the *Wesleyan Theological Journal*. This is a publication of the Wesleyan Theological Society, an organization which is largely composed of scholars from conservative Wesleyan denominations.

Not surprisingly, one issue which has received a good deal of attention in the *Journal* is Biblical authority. As in other conservative circles, there has been a good deal of discussion of the nature of Biblical inspiration and the role of Biblical criticism. The topic which has received most attention, however, is the Wesleyan doctrine of entire sanctification or Christian perfection.

In the past few years, especially, there has been extensive debate about the baptism of the Holy Spirit and how this relates to entire sanctification. Closely related is the question of glossolalia. Conservative Wesleyans have been notably cool toward glossolalia and have taken pains to deny that it is proof of the baptism of the Holy Spirit. Lately, however, there have been signs of openness toward glossolalia from some quarters of conservative Wesleyanism. But these issues are far from resolved, and the controversy is sure to continue.

It is not surprising that there is diversity within conservative Wesleyan circles on such matters as the nature of Biblical authority and the baptism of the Holy Spirit. Nor is theological controversy on such issues necessarily a bad thing. For controversy often provokes discussion which leads to a better understanding of the issues involved.

But what about more basic doctrine? Are not conservative Wesleyans firmly united at this point? Generally speaking, I think the answer to this question is yes. Nevertheless, some evidence indicates that this is not entirely the case. Consider, for example, a *Wesleyan Theological Journal* article written by John Culp entitled, "A Dialogue With the Process Theology of John B. Cobb, Jr."[20]

In this essay, Culp presents Cobb's process theology as a helpful model for interpreting Wesleyan theology. This is certainly an interesting proposal in view of the fact that Cobb, according to Culp, holds "that there are no fixed guidelines for determining what is a positive or negative, true or false, development of Christianity."[21] This view, obviously, is quite amenable to theological pluralism, even at the level of basic Christian doctrine.

Process theology has become fairly prevalent in mainstream denominations, including United Methodism (Cobb is a United Methodist), but it is somewhat surprising to see process thought embraced within more traditionally oriented groups. It would not be wise to jump to the conclusion that liberal theology has permeated conservative Wesleyan denominations to any large degree, and I do not mean to suggest that. But I do think growing diversity exists within conservative Wesleyan circles and that theological pluralism is likely to emerge as a serious issue for some of these groups in the near future.

It is my conviction that the broader Wesleyan tradition can learn a great deal from United Methodism's attempt to deal with the problem of theological pluralism. Indeed, I think United Methodism's approach to the problem can be instructive to others besides Wesleyans. Much of what I write in subsequent chapters will be relevant to the problem of pluralism as it has developed within other Christian denominations. But the following discussion will be especially pertinent to the various branches of the Wesleyan tradition and, most particularly, the United Methodist Church.

1

THE MANY FACES OF PLURALISM

From what I have written so far, one might assume that the meaning of pluralism is reasonably clear and that all sides in the controversy surrounding pluralism at least agree on what pluralism is. But this is not the case, as will be apparent in the next chapter where I take a careful look at how pluralism is presented in the United Methodist *Discipline*.

In the present chapter, however, I want to take the preliminary step of considering some of the different ways in which the concept of pluralism is commonly used in theological literature. My reason for doing this is simple, namely, because these uses of pluralism are often run together with the notion of *theological* pluralism in such a way that the issues being discussed are totally obscured. I want at the outset to sort out these various uses of the concept of pluralism in order to avoid as much confusion as possible in the following discussion. In other words, this brief chapter is an attempt to clear the decks before taking on those matters which will primarily concern us.

Pluralism and Politics

In the first place, the concept of pluralism is frequently invoked in the context of politics. In political theory, a fundamental difference exists between those who have a unitary view of society and those who have a pluralist view. Those who hold a unitary view see society as basically one and think in terms of a common good which pertains to all of society. For those who hold this view, the "role of politics is to discover and implement those public policies which reflect and meet the unified needs and interests of all of society."[1]

Those who hold the pluralist view also recognize certain basic values and beliefs which are held in common within a society. However, the political pluralist recognizes no one common good or public interest. Rather, society is composed of a vast range of groups—ethnic, racial, cultural, and so on—which represent a wide diversity of values, beliefs, and interests. Accordingly, the role of politics cannot be to discover and implement any one common good or public interest. Rather, "public policy is to be made by a bargaining, negotiating, compromising process in which the various groupings in pluralist society all have a say."[2] The pluralist model particularly recognizes the impact which minorities may make. For minorities epitomize the challenge to the assumption that there is one interest or good which is common to all.

The notion of pluralism as a political reality easily slips into discussions of United Methodist pluralism. Consider the following, which are the opening words of an article on the 1984 United Methodist episcopal elections.

> History may well record 1984 as the year the jurisdictional conferences took the pluralism of the church seriously. In 19 elections, the conferences chose two women, five black persons, one Hispanic and one Asian American.[3]

Episcopal elections are among the most politicized events in United Methodism, complete with caucuses, compromises, vote trade-offs and so on. Different special interest groups support different candidates and vie for as much influence as possible through episcopal channels.

This perspective comes through even more clearly in a later passage in the article.

> Granted the strength of these expressions of pluralism, it must be said also that the mood was not uniform. For a number of years many observers have felt that the South Central Jurisdiction, where the largest concentration of Hispanic United Methodists on the mainland is to be found, should have at least one Hispanic person in its College of Bishops. . . . but in the end the jurisdiction chose three white Anglo males.[4]

The assumption here seems to be that pluralism is taken seriously insofar as the pie of political power is properly sliced with respect to the numerous special interest groups in United Methodism. From this perspective, it is quite natural to slice the episcopal pie in such terms as women, blacks, Hispanics, Asian Americans, and white Anglo males. It is further suggested that bishops have a responsibility to faithfully represent the particular concerns of whatever special interest group they may be identified with.

The political aspect of pluralism is also reflected in a recent article by Bishop Woodie W. White. He begins by observing that: "The United Methodist Church is engaged in a tough but noble enterprise—the attainment of a racially inclusive and pluralistic denomination." While granting that the goal of full inclusiveness has not yet been reached, he emphasizes that significant progress has been made. One notable sign of this progress is that "ethnic minority representation in policy-making decisions is at an all-time high."[5] Again, it is suggested that true pluralism is something to be achieved. And one of the best means of achieving pluralism is by making sure that the several racial and ethnic minorities have a say at the policy-making level of the church.

Of course, there is nothing wrong with using the term "pluralism" in this sense. But when the context of discussion is pluralism in United Methodism, care needs to be taken to avoid misleading associations of the term.

Pluralism as Human Diversity

A second understanding of pluralism is rooted in the simple fact of human diversity. Of course, human diversity is also basic to pluralism conceived in political terms. The emphasis here, though, is not upon groups which represent competing interests but upon the more general reality that the human race is composed of a broad spectrum of types of people. Individuality is to be respected and celebrated. But it is not just the human race which reflects such diversity. The Christian Church, also, has always displayed the rich diversity which is typical of humanity. Pluralism, so understood, is affirmed in the following words of Bishop Emerson Colaw.

> . . .there is no theological party-line in our denomi-
> nation to which all must subscribe. . . . We therefore
> accept, as a part of our distinctive style, the fact that
> words such as diversity, pluralism, renewalist,
> evangelical, and new theologies are a part of our
> vocabulary as United Methodists. This concept of
> pluralism and diversity is as old as the Church. . . .
> The masses of people who met Jesus and were
> touched by him were not a homogenized crowd.
> They were shepherds and magi, taxgatherers and
> farmers, children and the influential, blind beggars

and generous women, in fact, representatives of every class in society and of every type conceivable in the moral order.[6]

What is particularly interesting about this passage is how the bishop runs together the idea of theological pluralism with the notion that pluralism is a matter of mere human diversity. He begins his chapter with a clear affirmation of theological pluralism. Within the space of a page, he is expounding upon the human diversity which has always characterized the Christian Church. The suggestion is that there is little more to affirming theological pluralism than accepting and affirming human diversity. Indeed, the impression conveyed is that theological pluralism is as natural and desirable as the different colors in a rainbow.

Certainly ethnic, racial, social, and cultural diversity are values to be celebrated and maintained. The United Methodist Church should certainly strive to exhibit such diversity, since the Gospel is for persons of all races and cultures. However, nothing but carelessness and confusion can result when this type of pluralism is lumped together with theological pluralism.

This is not to say that there is no connection whatever between racial and cultural pluralism and theological pluralism. As our *Discipline* says, in the context of affirming pluralism: "The invitation to theological reflection is open to all—young and old, unlettered and learned, persons of all cultures, ethnic groups, and races" (p. 73). Surely, theological pluralism is partially generated by the fact that persons of all these types have accepted the invitation to theological reflection. Nevertheless, the concept of theological pluralism must be clearly distinguished from the concept of pluralism as human diversity. The impression should not be given that if one appreciates and delights in human individuality and diversity, he thereby affirms theological pluralism.

Unity and Diversity in the Body of Christ

Another popular way of conceiving of pluralism is in terms of the New Testament image of the Church as the Body of Christ. Just as the human body has many different members which complement one another, so the different members of the Church have a variety of spiritual gifts for serving one another and the world. Richard G. Hutcheson Jr. appeals to this familiar picture in calling for evangelicals and theological liberals to accommodate one another in the mainline churches.

> There is . . . a theological model for the pluralistic church on which such accommodation can be based: the Biblical imagery of the one body with many members, one spirit with many gifts. While the church has never found the final answer to the problem of unity and diversity, Biblical patterns clearly suggest that some answer must be found, that both unity and diversity are inevitably present in the Body of Christ.[7]

This New Testament image is an attractive one to which believers readily resonate. This is particularly so in an age enlivened by the charismatic renewal, which has placed so much emphasis on spiritual gifts. That each member of the Body has at least one spiritual gift which is to be exercised for the benefit of others is a vital truth for the health of the Church. This truth underscores the fact that none of us can stand in proud independence or isolation. The various members of the Body need each other.

Furthermore, it is important for all spiritual gifts to be exercised if the Church is to have a holistic ministry. For example, the gift of evangelism is crucial, but evangelism is not the whole of ministry. It is also necessary for the gift of mercy to flourish if the hungry are to be fed. And the gift of prophecy must be stirred up if the complacency of both the Church and the world is to be challenged by the Biblical demand for justice and integrity. While the ministries of evangelism, mercy, and prophecy are surely distinct, they are also mutually supportive. The old dichotomy between evangelism and social action must be abandoned forever.

It is doubtful, however, whether the image of the Body of Christ is a helpful model for dealing with theological pluralism. For central to the image of the Body is the notion that the different members complement one another. Harmony prevails when the different gifts are functioning properly. But when we examine theological pluralism, it is not at all apparent that diverse theological views always complement one another. In actuality, some theological positions flatly contradict one another. This fact cannot be obscured by merely invoking the appealing image of the one Body with many members.

Pluralism, Christianity, and Other Religions

The concept of pluralism is becoming increasingly common in yet another context, namely, in discussions of the world religions. The idea of pluralism is not used here merely to acknowledge the existence of several such religions, but to emphasize a certain view of the relationship between the various religions. That view, as stated by John Hick—a leading proponent of the view—is that "at its best, each of the great world faiths constitutes a perception of and a response to the ultimate divine reality which they all in their different ways affirm." Hick goes on in the next paragraph to remark: "This view of humankind's religious life is sometimes called relativism, but is, I think, more appropriately called pluralism."[8]

Hick's claims thus far could be accepted by many orthodox Christians. Numerous Christian thinkers have suggested or explicitly argued that adherents of other religions, who have never heard the Christian Gospel, may have some genuine knowledge of God, and may in fact be saved. Among this number, interestingly, is John Wesley, who held open the possibility that the "heathen," though without explicit knowledge of the way of salvation through Christ, may be saved.[9]

Hick, however, wants to go much farther than this. For him, to affirm pluralism with respect to the world religions is to deny that Christianity has a unique place among those religions. Yet, Hick recognizes that traditional Christian doctrine poses a serious problem for his proposal.

> The older theological tradition of Christianity does not readily permit religious pluralism. For at its center is the conviction that Jesus of Nazareth was God—the Second Person of a Divine Trinity living a human life. It follows from this that Christianity, and Christianity alone, was founded by God in person on the only occasion on which he has ever become incarnate in this world, so that Christianity has a unique status as the way of salvation provided and appointed by God himself.[10]

The problem described here is that the most central doctrines of Christianity involve truth claims which stand in the way of any attempt to make Christianity fit Hick's theory of religious pluralism.

However, Hick has a way to deal with this difficulty. Following the fashion of much modern and contemporary theology, he argues that such traditional doctrines as the Incarnation and the Resurrection must be interpreted metaphorically or mythically. That is, we must give up thinking that it is factually true that "Jesus was God the Son incarnate." Indeed, Hick would have us think the formal development of orthodox Christology was a mistake, though an understandable one.

According to his reading of the tradition, Jesus was gradually deified over a period of time. This happened

largely under the impact of the early Christians'
experience of finding reconciliation with God through
encountering Christ. The death of Christ was central to
their experience of reconciliation, and the early disciples
naturally reached the conclusion that if Jesus' death
could atone for sin, He must be divine.

The notion that Jesus was the Son of God, according to
Hick, was originally understood poetically. It was only
natural, however, "that later this poetry should have
hardened into prose, and escalated from a metaphorical
son of God to a metaphysical God the Son, of the same
substance as the Father within the triune Godhead."[11]
But since this doctrine is "devoid of meaning" when
understood literally, it is appropriate to construe it
otherwise.

> It therefore seems reasonable to conclude that the
> real point and value of the incarnation doctrine is
> not indicative but expressive, not to assert a
> metaphysical fact, but to express a valuation and
> evoke an attitude. . . . I suggest that its character is
> best expressed by saying that the idea of divine
> incarnation is a mythological idea. And I am using
> the term "myth" in the following sense: a myth is a
> story which is told but which is not literally true, or
> an idea or image which is applied to someone or
> something but which does not literally apply, but
> which invites a particular attitude in its hearers. . . .
> In the case of Jesus it gives definitive expression to
> his efficacy as savior from sin and ignorance and as
> giver of new life; it offers a way of declaring his
> significance to the world; and it expresses a disciple's
> commitment to Jesus as his personal Lord. He is the
> one in following whom we have found ourselves in
> God's presence and have found God's meaning for
> our lives.[12]

It is easy to see how this interpretation of the Incarnation strips the Christian faith of its unique claims. Although Jesus was not actually God incarnate He was remarkably aware of God, and others may come to a deeper knowledge of God through Him. This understanding of Jesus makes it relatively easy for Hick to fit Christianity into his mosaic of religious pluralism.

However, Hick's method of dealing with traditional Christian doctrine obviously raises serious questions. Indeed, I have quoted at length and gone into some detail here precisely because the issues raised by Hick will be central in our discussion of theological pluralism in the next chapter.

That is not to say that the matter of religious pluralism, which we have been treating here, is exactly the same as the matter of theological pluralism. Theological pluralism, as I shall be dealing with it, is restricted to theological diversity which is internal to only one of the great world religions, namely, Christianity. That is, theological pluralism is concerned with the relationship between diverse interpretations of Christianity rather than with the relationship between Christianity and other world faiths.

However, some of the basic philosophical and theological issues are the same in both discussions. For instance, the nature of theological language is a fundamental question common to discussions of both religious pluralism and theological pluralism. Does theological language make factual claims which must be maintained, even if those claims contradict truth claims of other religions or theological traditions? Or can such apparently factual claims be interpreted metaphorically in order to eliminate contradictions? We shall return to these questions in the next chapter.

Concluding Comments

There are still other ways of applying the concept of pluralism, and some of these are relevant to theological pluralism. My purpose here has not been to cite all such applications, but only to highlight the fact that the concept of pluralism is used in a number of ways in contemporary theological and ecclesiastical literature. Of course, there is nothing illegitimate about using the term in these various senses, and I do not mean to imply otherwise. Pluralism is simply another word for diversity and can be properly applied in any number of contexts. On the other hand, nothing but misunderstanding can result when these other uses are carelessly lumped together with the concept of theological pluralism.

My purpose here has been achieved if the reader is sufficiently warned to beware of such confusions when the topic of theological pluralism is under discussion. With this preliminary task behind us, we can turn now to examine theological pluralism itself.

2

WHAT IS THEOLOGICAL PLURALISM?

I have already indicated that there is no easy answer to the question I am posing in this chapter. Compounding the confusion generated when the concept of theological pluralism is lumped together with other notions of pluralism is the fact that there has never been a clear understanding of theological pluralism itself. A number of conservative United Methodist spokesmen have made this point in recent years.

James Heidinger, for example, argues that theological pluralism has never been adequately defined, despite the fact that a definition for doctrinal pluralism has appeared in the glossary of the United Methodist *Discipline*. As Heidinger points out, that definition was not part of the 1972 General Conference legislation. Indeed the definition "was not placed into the *Discipline* by legislation and careful General Conference action, but was added after the 1976 General Conference." Heidinger goes on to comment: "Characteristic of our theological confusion, a General Conference voted overwhelmingly to accept a concept that was without definition."[1]

Another indication of confusion is the fact that the *Discipline* uses the terms "theological pluralism" and "doctrinal pluralism" interchangeably, with no apparent distinction in mind. The definition in the glossary, as I have noted, is for doctrinal pluralism, but what was affirmed as a principle in 1972 was theological pluralism. The failure to distinguish between these terms suggests that doctrine and theology are the same. I shall argue in a later chapter that they are not. (In the meantime I shall follow the *Discipline* in using the terms interchangeably.)

The main purpose of the present chapter is to seek a clear understanding of the concept of theological pluralism. I will focus my analysis on the definition which was added to our *Discipline* in 1976. The definition also appears in the 1980 *Discipline,* but was dropped from the 1984 *Discipline,* along with the rest of the glossary. Despite questions concerning the way this definition was added to the *Discipline,* and has now disappeared, it still deserves examination to determine whether it is a viable definition. My examination of the definition will be carried out in the light of Part II of our *Discipline,* which deals with Doctrine and Doctrinal Statements.

Analyzing the Definition

Here, then, is the glossary definition of doctrinal pluralism.

> Expounded thoroughly in Wesley's famous sermon "Catholic Spirit," an attitude toward Christian truth that, recognizing the limitations of language, allows for more than one verbal statement of truth, each statement pointing to the truth but not exhausting truth nor excluding all other expressions of truth. This principle maintains the continuity and identity of the Christian message but assumes that this may find legitimate expression in various theological "systems" or in special interest theologies. Differ-

ences may be argued fruitfully in terms of evidence and cogency (*Discipline*, 1980, p. 651).

The initial reaction one is likely to have after reading this definition is to wonder why theological pluralism is considered to be such a source of confusion. The definition seems straightforward and rather clear. And furthermore, if theological pluralism is an idea which comes straight from Wesley, we may wonder why conservatives have been so critical of it. For the definition purports to be merely a summary of Wesley's exposition of catholic spirit.

In the next chapter I want to examine Wesley's sermon on catholic spirit in light of the *Discipline's* definition of pluralism, but for now I want to emphasize that this definition embodies a number of other substantial claims. For the sake of clarity, let us separate these as follows.

1) Language is limited as a vehicle for expressing truth.
2) In recognition of this, pluralism allows for more than one verbal statement of Christian truth.
3) Each such statement points to the truth, but none can exhaust it.
4) No one statement of Christian truth can exclude all other such statements.
5) The Christian message has a recognizable identity, so there is continuity between various verbal expressions of it.
6) This identity and continuity may be maintained in various theological systems and special interest theologies.
7) When various theological systems and special interest theologies conflict with one another, the differences may be argued in terms of evidence and cogency.

When the definition is broken down in this fashion, it becomes evident that theological pluralism is not so simple a matter as it might first appear. Indeed, our definition embraces a number of important philosophical and theological issues. These involve the nature of language, the nature of truth, the identity of the Christian message, and the continuity of that message in various verbal expressions of it. The remainder of this chapter will be concerned with these issues.

Language and Truth

When we enter the territory of language and truth, we are entering an arena of great complexity and involved debate in recent philosophy. It would take us far astray even to begin to discuss these issues in detail. However, we must engage them to some extent in order to deal honestly with the issues raised by the definition of pluralism which we are considering. As our analysis above has already made clear, considerations about the nature of language and its relation to truth are central to that definition. Proposition 1 is the basic premise, and propositions 2-4 enlarge on this. The remaining propositions also involve these issues, but in a less obvious way.

How then is language related to truth? How is language related to reality? Let us begin to approach these matters by considering the following lines of Roger Trigg.

> If language can be used as a means of communication (and the writing of this sentence assumes that this is so) certain presuppositions must be built into it. . . . What is of supreme importance is that there is some notion of truth as such in human language. This is the cement which binds language together. . . . Because a main function of language is to talk about and communicate what is the case, the absence of any distinction between truth and falsity

(i.e. between what is and is not so) will destroy language. [2]

The notion that there is a distinction between truth and falsity involves another assumption, namely, that there is a world of reality distinct from our language, which is the standard for distinguishing true and false statements.

This point accords with the observation that truth has two senses:

1) actual states of affairs, reality; and
2) true beliefs, judgments, propositions, etc.[3]

The first sense of truth is ontological. It has to do with what exists, what happened, what the facts are, etc. The second sense of truth is epistemological and linguistic. That is, it has to do with how we come to know and express the truth.

Notice that these two distinct senses of truth seem to be assumed in the *Discipline's* definition of pluralism. This is especially apparent in the statement that pluralism "allows for more than one verbal statement of truth [i.e. truth in sense 2], each statement pointing to the truth [i.e. truth in sense 1] but not exhausting truth."

Notice also that truth in sense 2 is dependent upon and controlled by truth in sense 1. That is, true judgments and propositions are not to be confused with the reality they describe. Rather, their function is to be a medium of conveying or revealing what is actual and real. As T.F. Torrance puts it: "For a true statement to serve the truth of being, it must fall short of it, be revisable in the light of it, and not be mistaken for it, since it does not possess its truth in itself but in the reality it serves. Thus, a dash of inadequacy is necessary for its precision."[4]

So the important thing is to realize there is a close connection between the truth of true statements and the truth of reality, but that they are not identical. It is in this sense that we must recognize a "dash of inadequacy" in our most precise statements. We must be careful, however, not to overstate the inadequacy of language, or we remove any basis for assuming it is a sufficient vehicle even to point to truth. Language is perfectly adequate to point to the truth, to make true statements about it, but it is inadequate as a substitute for the truth it conveys.

A stress upon the inadequacy of language undergirds our *Discipline's* definition of pluralism. This definition is based on the assumption that, because statements about the truth are not to be identified with the truth, more than one verbal statement of the truth may be allowed. No one statement of the truth can exclude all others because the reality which a statement points to may not only permit, but even require, other statements if it is to be fully (but not exhaustively) expressed. Moreover, different statements may say essentially the same thing.[5]

Christian theologians have, for centuries, recognized the validity of these points. Indeed, the classic illustration of these points is the Nicene Creed. For the heart of that creed, the affirmation that Christ is *homoousios* (of one substance) with the Father, is an expression of Biblical truth in extra-Biblical language.

> All that Nicaea did was to reduce the multiplicity of the Scriptural affirmations to the unity of a single affirmation. . . . Therefore it was nothing new. . . . The Nicene dogma was new, however, in that it stated the sense of the Scriptures in a new mode of understanding that was not formally Scriptural. The Scriptures had affirmed that Jesus Christ, the Son, is here with us as Lord of us. Nicaea affirmed that the Lord Jesus Christ is the consubstantial Son. The sense of both affirmations is the same, but the mode of conception and statement is different.[6]

So the Nicene Creed is a major example of theologizing which recognizes that the limitations of language not only allow, but sometimes even require, more than one verbal statement of truth if the truth in question is to be accurately expressed.

The Nicene *homoousion* was required because Arius had raised the question of who Christ is in Himself and in relation to the Father. Is Christ the same substance as the Father, and therefore God, or is He a creature? It was the conviction of the Nicene fathers that the language of Scripture discloses that the Son of God is a person who is properly described, in ontological terms, as *homoousios* with the Father. In affirming the *homoousion,* the fathers repudiated the notion that the Son of God is a creature, who had a beginning. For the Son cannot be both a creature who had a beginning and an eternal person, who is one substance with the Father.

This illustrates the important point that different verbal expressions which purport to point to the same truth or reality must be consistent with each other if each is to be recognized as a true statement. Such statements must complement one another or illuminate different facets of the same truth. Thus, if one accepts the Nicene formula, one must believe it is consistent with the statements of Scripture and contributes to a fuller understanding of who Christ is.

Conversely, if different statements which purport to describe the same truth are plainly contradictory, as in the case of the Nicene formula and the views of Arius, one of them must be rejected as false. Otherwise, language cannot communicate what is true concerning the reality in question. When this occurs, as Trigg pointed out, one of the main functions of language is destroyed. Our *Discipline's* definition of pluralism apparently recognizes this distinction between truth and falsity, for it cites "cogency" as one of the criteria for dealing with differences.

Thus far, then, it appears the *Discipline's* definition of pluralism has solid philosophical grounding, for it is based upon a longstanding and widely accepted account of language and truth. It should be accentuated that this account of language is clearly cognitive. That is to say, it aims to describe the facts, or tell us what is the case. It is related to objective reality in such a way that it points to reality and truly expresses it.

This view of theological language is not unusual or esoteric. Rather, it is the implicit understanding of such language assumed by most believers. I emphasize it, however, because various non-cognitive views of theolgocial language have been influential in much contemporary theology and philosophy of religion. This, again, is a very complex field of inquiry which we cannot fully explore. But it is important to be clear on the fact that many contemporary theologians reject the apparent meaning of traditional theological claims. In the last chapter, we saw a good example of this approach in John Hick's mythical interpretation of the Incarnation.

Such interpretations grant that statements like "God created the world" and "God raised Christ from the dead" appear to be factual assertions informing us of the existence and activity of a Being who transcends the natural world. However, the argument goes, if such claims are to be retained in our day, they must be given a more mundane meaning. Writers who hold such views typically resort to reductionism in their analysis of classical theological statements. That is, they reduce statements about God and alleged supernatural events merely to claims about man and his experience. Consider, for instance, how the doctrine of Creation might be handled.

Once one has adopted a reductionist theology and has restricted one's attention to the influence of religion on men's lives, it becomes impossible to talk of a personal God or a Creator. A statement such as "God created the universe" can no longer be treated as true (or false), if this is understood as saying something about the origins of the universe. It has to be translated into some statement about the attitudes of those who believe it. For example, D.Z. Phillips says: "To see the world as God's creation is to see meaning in life. . . ." Statements which appear to be about God are in this way shown to be about believers.[7]

A similar kind of reductionism can be applied to statements of belief in Christ's resurrection. Such statements would not be understood as referring to an actual event in the past in which God raised Christ from the dead. Rather, affirmations of the Resurrection might be interpreted "in terms of 'a new perspective upon life' opened up for the apostles and modern man."[8]

Understood along these lines, the story of the Resurrection could be said to be true in the mythical sense which Hick applies to the Incarnation. That is, it is not literally true that Jesus was raised from the dead. However, the story of the Resurrection "invites a particular attitude in its hearers." It invites those who hear it to recognize Jesus' significance for the world and encourages commitment to Him.

This kind of analysis of traditional theological language may strike some as contrived and distorted. Why is it necessary to resort to such measures? The answer is that these writers, while rejecting traditional views of God, the supernatural, and revelation, still want to call themselves Christians. They do not believe that classical creedal affirmations are true as traditionally understood, but still want to insist that in some other sense Christianity remains true.

At bottom then, these different views of theological language reflect fundamentally different understandings of theological truth and accordingly, of the Christian faith. The depth of this difference must not be underestimated. As William J. Abraham put it, "The abandoning of factual discourse about direct divine action is a momentous step to take. Indeed, so momentous that it will destroy the Christian tradition as it is generally known."[9] Let us keep these points in mind as we go on to consider the remainder of our *Discipline's* definition of theological pluralism.

Identity and Continuity

As we recall, the *Discipline's* definition of pluralism "maintains the continuity and identity of the Christian message." The issues of identity and continuity are no less difficult than the issues of language and truth which we have been considering. Indeed, they are further aspects of these problems. So we must continue to proceed with care.

Let us begin with a working definition of *identity.* Identity refers to the characteristics or criteria by which something or someone is known, recognized, or distinguished. These characteristics or criteria are what enable us to identify or "pick out" a person or thing from among other persons or things.

The concept of identity is crucial for the concept of continuity. The only way we can know whether the Christian message has continued is if we can identify it. To say the Christian message has continued is to say that it is, in some sense, the same message today which the early Church proclaimed. The idea of sameness is the basis for continuity. As Paul Holmer put it, "the core of theology for Protestants, not only Catholics, is a divine 'magesterium' which is the same from age to age."[10]

This much may seem fairly obvious. However, when we look more closely at the ideas of identity, continuity, and sameness, we must reckon with some notorious difficulties. For instance, the word "same" is inherently ambiguous. Consider some examples of how it is used: (1) All of us went to the same movie last night. (2) Those two men are wearing the same tie. (3) This is the same school it was one hundred years ago. (4) All the speakers at the conference said the same thing.

It is apparent, I think, from these examples that the

word "same" has both a strict as well as a loose sense. The question for us is, how strictly must the word be used in order to maintain the identity and continuity of the Christian message? What does it mean to say the Christian message is the same from age to age, from theological system to theological system, and from one special-interest theology to another?

One thing it cannot mean is that the Christian message is exactly identical in all these cases. Basil Mitchell makes this point nicely with a question: "When Augustine returned to the faith in which Monica had nurtured him, must we deny that he remained in the *same* faith, if he went on to explore its implications in directions that Monica had never thought of?"[11]

This quote from Mitchell highlights one reason why Christian truth is expressed in different ways, namely, because different theologians have explored its implications in different directions. Certainly no single person is capable of drawing out all the riches implicit in the Christian faith. Different thinkers will quite appropriately unfold, emphasize, and apply various facets of the Gospel in very diverse circumstances. Their own experience will often be a major factor giving shape to their particular insights and emphases. None of this should come as a surprise or strike us as objectionable.

Yet, we are still without an adequate answer as to what is the identity of the Christian message which enables us to say that different expressions of it are indeed, in a real sense, the "same." If we have not identified the Christian message, how can we recognize genuine instances of continuity? What are the criteria for identifying the Christian message? What is essential to it?

The answer which suggests itself most readily is that the essential things are set forth in the ecumenical creeds.[12] This answer has a number of points in its favor. In the first place is the simple fact that the doctrines of the creeds have been time-tested points of agreement among all three branches of the Christian Church:

Roman Catholic, Eastern Orthodox, and Protestant. The Nicene Creed, especially, has been universally accepted.

Yet, there is more to this point than the simple historical fact of the universal appeal of the creeds. We have to ask whether there is even any other plausible answer to the question of Christian identity. If the creeds do not truly state essential Christian doctrine, can we ever hope to know the identity of the Christian message? If the Church catholic has been mistaken for centuries in its insistence upon the doctrines of the creeds, are we not driven to the conclusion that the meaning of God's revelation, which the creeds attempt to state, is hopelessly beyond us?

For the very idea that God has revealed Himself assumes that the meaning of that revelation is accessible to us. It has been the confidence of Christians for centuries that the Church, under the guidance of the Holy Spirit, correctly understood and stated the meaning of God's revelation in the creeds.

There is another reason for accepting the creeds as definitive statements of essential Christian doctrine, namely, because they clearly have an ontological reference. That is, they tell us the identity of the realities to which the Christian message points. They tell us who God is and identify the events through which God has revealed Himself.

The miraculous events cited in the creeds, the Virginal Conception, the Resurrection, and the Ascension are vital to the Christian message because of their connection to the Incarnation. It was the Resurrection, above all, which disclosed that Christ is an eternal person who, therefore, could not be held by death. The Virginal Conception should also be viewed in the light of who Christ is, as revealed by the Resurrection. As T.F. Torrance puts it, "the Resurrection discloses that the Virgin Birth was the act and mode of the Creator's entry into his own creation as Man among men."[13] Likewise, the Ascension discloses who Christ is, for it was the event in which He returned to the glory of His Father, which He laid aside in the Incarnation. In short, these events are essential because they disclose who Christ is: the eternal Son of God who became incarnate for our salvation.

This suggests that the key to knowing the identity of the Christian message is knowing the identity of the realities to which the message points. If we have an accurate (though not exhaustive) account of who God is, and how He has revealed Himself, we have firm grounds for maintaining the continuity of the Christian message. If we know something about the identity of Christ, for instance, (which is the main contention of the Nicene Creed) we know something which will not change. As the book of Hebrews puts is: "Jesus Christ is the same yesterday and today and forever" (13:8, NIV).

It is important to emphasize, however, that what is definitive is the truth which is expressed by the creeds, not the particular expressions used to convey that truth. That is to say, the Nicene formula for instance, may be restated in different language. Indeed, this may be necessary if the truth of the creed is to be effectively communicated to many contemporary believers. To say this is only to recognize a fundamental premise of the Nicene fathers themselves: that it is sometimes necessary to employ new expressions in order to maintain old truths.

One may object, regarding this emphasis on the creeds, that the Christian message is much more than a series of statements of fact, if it is that at all. The Christian message also concerns life, here and now, by making possible a new way of living.

My intention has not been to deny that the Christian message concerns a way of life. Indeed, the view I have defended undergirds this claim. For the Christian life is very much tied to the identity of Christ and the events of His life.

Anthony Thiselton underscores this point by commenting on the "concern for orthodoxy" which has been so prominent in the Christian tradition.

> What is at stake is whether the Christian way is
> turned into "another gospel" (Galatians 1:8). The
> concern which is expressed appears quite other than
> negative and restrictive when it is seen that what is at
> issue is the maintenance of that degree of continuity
> which is necessary for Christian *identity* and more
> especially for participation in the *patterns of behavior
> which have been instituted and prescribed* by those events
> on which the community itself has been founded.[14]

Thiselton recognizes that to speak of patterns of
behavior or "roles" may seem to reduce authentic
Christian faith to a mere routine. He goes on, however,
to insist that:

> Christian believing involves taking up certain
> *patterns* of attitudes and behavior which can be said
> to be recognizably "Christian" precisely because they
> are patterns. . . . Because of God's saving acts in
> Christ, the status of "son," or "one of the redeemed"
> (and so on) may now be offered and accepted, and
> the role of the worshipper, obedient servant (and so
> on) "taken over" or appropriated. For all this to be
> meaningful, however, there *must* be a relatively
> stable background of repetition, habituation, or
> "expected" belief and conduct.[15]

So the creeds and early confessions should not be seen as
something which stifle authentic Christian faith and
experience. Rather, they are essential for its preserva-
tion. As Thiselton puts it, the creeds mediate "to later
generations the corporate knowledge and memory on
which the authenticity of faith" depends.[16]

Thus, to maintain Christian identity, and continuity in
what it means to live the Christian life, we must maintain
continuity in our understanding of the events upon

which the Christian community is founded.

Identity, Continuity, and Special-interest Theologies

Now that we have considered the meaning of identity and continuity, we can go on to evaluate the claim that the Christian message "may find legitimate expression in various theological 'systems' or in special-interest theologies" (*Discipline*, 1980, p. 651).

As a general statement, I think this claim must be accepted without quibble. The history of theology provides ample evidence that the Christian message has been powerfully expressed in a multitude of theological systems. We need not go beyond the names of Aquinas, Luther, Calvin, Cranmer, and Wesley to be reminded of this point. The various traditions represented by these men differ in a number of respects. And yet, without downplaying the differences, we can properly emphasize that there is a definite core of agreement between these various theologies. The doctrines of the ecumenical creeds are basic to all. Thus it is possible to have substantial doctrinal unity in the midst of real theological diversity.[17]

This much, I think, is fairly clear. But of course, the claim we are considering goes beyond these relatively easy cases. The difficulty arises when we come to some of the more recent theological systems and special-interest theologies. It is not so simple then to agree that all of them are expressions of the "same" Christian message.

As our Doctrinal Statement notes, "the theological spectrum in the United Methodist Church ranges over all the current mainstream options and a variety of special-interest theologies as well" (p. 73). The concept of pluralism apparently lends legitimacy to the entire spectrum. We cannot here even enumerate all these theologies. However, we need to have some idea of what our Doctrinal Statement means by "special-interest theologies." We can make some headway in this direction by examining the section of our Statement entitled "Theological Frontiers and New Directions."

In the first place, our Statement singles out for mention theologies of liberation. "Notable among them are black theology, female liberation, political and ethnic theologies, third-world theology, and theologies of human rights" (p. 82). A paragraph later, other examples are cited.

> The United Methodist Church also takes seriously other widely variant theological emphases of our time . . . We witness recurring expressions of neo-fundamentalism, new pentecostalism, new forms of Christian naturalism and secularity (p. 83).

This gives us some idea of what "special-interest theologies" are, and puts us in a better position to evaluate the claim that they, too, are legitimate expressions of the Christian message.

However, before we do so, let us take into account a few more lines from this section of the Doctrinal Statement which bear on special-interest theologies.

> All claims to Christian truth deserve an open and fair hearing for their sifting and assessment. The viability of all doctrinal opinion demands that the processes of theological development must be kept open ended, both on principle and in fact (p. 83).

I will analyze this passage in detail in a subsequent chapter, but I cite it here because it represents a very interesting rationale for the legitimacy of special-interest theologies.

We must realize what this passage is saying. The key clause, I think, is: "The viability of all doctrinal opinion demands that the processes of theological development must be kept open ended." This forces a number of questions. Are *all* doctrinal opinions viable? What about doctrinal opinions which contradict basic Christian beliefs? If the Christian message has an identity, does this not place some limitations on theological development? Let us keep these questions in mind as we turn our focus back to the special-interest theologies mentioned in our Doctrinal Statement. What about the claim that all of these may be legitimate expressions of the Christian message?

Some of the examples cited pose no great problem. Theologies of liberation, for example, may certainly give legitimate expression to the message of the Gospel. One may hold fast to the essential doctrines of Christianity while accenting and developing the idea that Christ brings liberation in all phases of life.[18] A similar assessment holds with respect to neofundamentalism and new pentecostalism. Since both are committed to the basic doctrines of orthodox theology, while placing distinct emphases on different facets of the Christian message, there is good reason to hold that each of them maintains the identity and continuity of the Christian message.

However, when we come to the other examples cited, namely, Christian naturalism and secularity, a number of problems come immediately to the fore. For the sake of simplicity, I will limit my discussion to naturalism.

The most obvious question which must be faced is how the identity of the Christian message can be maintained in naturalism. If our discussion thus far has been on track at all, it is obvious that *supernaturalism* is essential to the identity of the Christian message. That is, the Christian message maintains the actual existence of a supernatural Being and the factuality of certain supernatural events through which this Being has revealed Himself. These events, traditionally called miracles, involve God's intervention in the natural order. As William Abraham put it, "it is clear that some of the acts traditionally attributed to God in the doctrine of special revelation were, if they occurred, violations of laws of nature."[19] It is

such acts of divine intervention, however, which cannot
be allowed by naturalism, even if it is called "Christian"
naturalism.

How, then, can naturalism be Christian? Is the identity
of Christian truth actually such that a naturalistic system
can express it?

In response to this question, let us recall our discussion
above in which we dealt briefly with noncognitive
analyses of theological language. As we saw, a number of
theologians have argued that we may still affirm such
things as Creation and the Resurrection without affirming the traditional understanding of them. The story of
the Resurrection, let us say, may transform our attitude
toward life, and in this sense redeem us, even if we do not
actually believe God intervened in the natural order to
raise Christ from the dead. Thus, it may be argued, the
Resurrection is not denied, it is merely given a different
interpretation than in classical theology.

The idea of interpretation is the key. Consider the
following lines from our Doctrinal Statement.

> There is a core of doctrine which informs in greater
> or less degree our widely divergent interpretations.
> From our response in faith to the wondrous mystery
> of God's love in Jesus Christ as recorded in
> Scripture, all valid Christian doctrine is born. This is
> the touchstone by which all Christian teaching may
> be tested (p. 73).

Notice in this passage the emphasis on "our response."
Apparently this is the basis for "our widely divergent
interpretations," for there have been markedly diverse
responses to "God's love in Jesus Christ as recorded in
Scripture."

However, the question which arises from this passage
is: How can our response to God's love in Christ be the
source for all Christian doctrine, since some of our
responses conflict with others? In these cases, whose

response is to test whose? Are all responses to be accepted as valid interpretations of doctrine? How such questions are to be answered is entirely unclear.

In traditional theology, the situation is quite different. There the emphasis is on God's revelation, not our response. The test for Christian doctrine is whether it is true to that revelation. To recall our earlier discussion, the ontological truth of Christianity is the standard for judging verbal expressions of that truth, i.e. theology. The assumption here is that God has revealed Himself and His purposes in such a way that the recipients of that revelation accurately perceived it. Furthermore, Scripture is the product of that revelation, so that we have in it a true account of who God is, and how He has revealed Himself. Therefore, Scripture has been recognized in classical theology as the touchstone for testing Christian teaching.[20]

What I want to emphasize is that in the quote above, with its accent on "our response" as the vital element in doctrinal formulation, we have a shift away from traditional concepts of doctrinal criteria. But there is more—we also seem to have a shift in doctrinal content. For it is not clear whether the essential subject matter for Christian doctrine is God, or our response to God.

This brings us back to the question of the nature of theological language. Does it refer to objective reality, or is it only about human experience? When we talk about the Resurrection, for instance, are we talking about an event in which God actually raised Jesus from the dead? Or are we talking only about our response to Christ? That is, is it legitimate to "interpret" the Resurrection in terms of a "new perspective upon life," opened by the life of Christ, even if we do not believe Christ was raised in His body?

It is my judgment that our Doctrinal Statement leaves the way open for such reductionistic interpretations of classical theological affirmations. If this conclusion seems overdrawn, let us recall that the central question in this phase of our discussion is how "Christian natural-ism" can be considered a viable theological option. If naturalism is to be called "Christian," it must affirm Christian doctrine in some sense. Since traditional Christian doctrine is simply incompatible with natural-ism, it can only be possible for naturalism to affirm some version of Christianity which interprets supernatural elements in a reductionistic way.

But what becomes of the identity of the Christian message if supernatural events are given a reductionistic interpretation? Is there enough continuity between the Nicene Creed and Christian naturalism that we can say the identity of the Christian message is maintained in the latter?

The only way it seems possible to maintain continuity here is to argue that the identity of the Christian message is different than has been believed in traditional theology. It has been believed, for instance, that the bodily resurrection of Christ is essential, whereas the really essential thing is the new perspective on life which Christ opened up. If this is admitted, it can be held that there is continuity between traditional theology, and Christian naturalism. For traditional theology, while insisting on the Resurrection as a factual event, would agree that the resurrection of Christ opened a new perspective on life. In traditional theology, having a new perspective on life is a *consequence* of believing in the Resurrection, but believing in the Resurrection cannot be reduced to having such a new perspective on life. Reductionist theology, on the other hand, wants to keep the consequence of believing in the Resurrection while rejecting the Resurrection itself.

Notice, however, what has happened to the concept of continuity here. Modern interpretations, instead of traditional understandings, have become decisive in defining continuity. In other words, continuity is said to exist not because modern theologies agree with tradi-tional theology in identifying essential Christian doctrines but because traditional doctrines have been interpreted in ways which are compatible with modern viewpoints.

In short, if we are to accept Christian naturalism as a legitimate expression of the Christian message, we must redefine what it means to maintain the "continuity and identity of the Christian message." And this in turn requires a different understanding of pluralism than that which is based on the understanding of identity and continuity we discussed in the preceding sections of this chapter.

Conclusion

Our major finding in this chapter has been that our *Discipline* expresses at least two distinct understandings of theological pluralism. The first, which is spelled out in the definition from the glossary, is essentially that *the same truth may be stated in different verbal forms.* The second view is best summed up in the claim that *all doctrinal opinion is viable.* This view is demanded because our Doctrinal Statement allows that the identity of the Christian message may be maintained in such unlikely places as naturalism and secularity.

So this second understanding of pluralism is far more sweeping in its claims than the first. It permits not only different verbal expressions of Christian truth and different theological emphases, but even radical disagreement as to what is ontologically true at the very foundations of Christian doctrine. Thus it is not surprising that our *Discipline* draws no clear distinction between theological pluralism and doctrinal pluralism. In the final analysis, both are given full license. What this ultimately means is that the identity of the Christian message is left an open question.

At the outset of this chapter, I raised the question of whether pluralism is as confused a notion as its critics have charged. In view of our preceding discussion, I think we are constrained to admit that the charge of confusion is fully justified.

This means the United Methodist Church is characterized by enormous theological variety, but we have no clear rationale for it. It is not even clear what we mean by pluralism, let alone whether it is a sound idea.

> A Christian church which is aware of a wide variety of diverse theological positions and which deliberately decides not to adopt one of them, but rather to tolerate diversity, still has to offer a definite reason for doing so and to justify that reason in the face of objection. . . . Toleration of diversity itself needs to be justified theologically if it is to be able to claim any kind of integrity.[21]

Thus, it is a pressing challenge for United Methodism not only to define pluralism more clearly, but also to justify it theologically.

3

JOHN WESLEY AND
THEOLOGICAL PLURALISM

It is evident that one of the aims of the 1972 Doctrinal
Statement was to establish the point that the acceptance
of theological pluralism is nothing new in the United
Methodist tradition. We have already noted that the
definition of doctrinal pluralism in the glossary of the
Discipline purports to be merely a summary of Wesley's
sermon, "Catholic Spirit."

In addition, a number of passages in the Statement
itself convey the impression that the affirmation of
doctrinal pluralism has been a part of the United
Methodist heritage from its inception. On the very first
page of the Statement, which begins with a section on
historical background, it is asserted that the pioneers of
the tradition—the Wesleys, Albright, Otterbein,
Boehm—had only a "minimal" interest in dogma and
allowed for a "decent latitude" in the interpretation of
Christian truth (p. 40). Indeed, the Statement maintains,
these pioneers "were fully committed to the principles of
religious toleration and doctrinal pluralism" (pp. 40-41).

Later, in the section of the Statement entitled "Our

51

Theological Task," contemporary pluralism is again identified with the notion of "catholic spirit."

> . . . the theological spectrum in the United Method-
> ist Church ranges over all the current mainstream
> options and a variety of special-interest theologies as
> well. *This is no new thing.* Our founders supported
> what Wesley called "catholic spirit," which also
> prevails in much contemporary ecumenical theolo-
> gy (p. 73, *italics mine*).

The implication of this paragraph is obvious. If the contemporary theological scene exemplifies Wesley's catholic spirit, then those who are critical of it are out of step with Wesley and the United Methodist heritage.

The aim of this chapter is to examine the claim that Wesley's thought supports the modern notion of theological pluralism. I will analyze his sermon on catholic spirit in some detail in order to determine whether it is faithfully represented in the definition from the glossary of our *Discipline*. I will begin by taking a general look at Wesley's views on such topics as orthodoxy, heresy, and the value of right belief in the Christian life.

Wesley on Orthodoxy and Heresy

Wesley's theological lenience is well known. It was particularly notable for the age in which he lived, and he took pride in pointing out how broad was the foundation on which Methodism was built.

> There is no other religious society under heaven
> which requires nothing of men in order to their
> admission into it, but a desire to save their souls. . . .
> The Methodists alone do not insist on your holding
> this or that opinion; but they think and let think. . . .
> Here is our glorying; and a glory peculiar to us.[1]

This passage sets the tone for Wesley's attitude toward orthodoxy. We would not expect him to be overly concerned with orthodox formulations of the faith. And he does not disappoint us.

Most of what Wesley said about orthodoxy was negative. Typical is his famous claim that "orthodoxy or right opinions is, at best, but a very slender part of religion, if it can be allowed to be any part of it at all."[2] While this remark is a good sample of what he thought about orthodoxy, it is also easily misconstrued. This is evident from the fact that he had to explain, as well as defend, the remark to several of his critics.[3]

Wesley defines orthodoxy here as "right opinions," and a key to understanding him at this point is to recall his well-known distinction between essential doctrine and opinion. That is to say, he wanted to mark a difference between belief in the basic truths of Christianity, on the one hand, and beliefs about secondary matters, on the other. The latter he termed "opinions." When Wesley speaks of orthodoxy, he means not only proper belief concerning central Christian doctrine but also precisely correct opinions on relatively minor tenets of the faith.

While this distinction is important, it is not altogether clear what should qualify as a matter of mere opinion. In one passage, Wesley defined an opinion as "whatever is compatible with love to Christ and a work of grace."[4] This definition is quite general and leaves us uncertain as to what sort of beliefs Wesley has in mind. Perhaps the best way to get clear on this is to consider some of the specific examples he gives. In one interesting list of opinions, he cites "several subjects of importance; such as the nature and use of the moral law, the eternal decrees of God, the sufficiency and efficacy of his grace, and the perseverance of his children."[5]

These examples of opinions were points of dispute between Wesley and the Lutherans and Calvinists. That he considered these "subjects of importance" is obvious from the strong opinions he expressed on these issues.[6] His attack on Calvinism is particularly noteworthy. And yet, he singled out Calvinistic opinions as examples of views which are "compatible with love to Christ, and a work of grace." So despite his strong views on these matters, he did not consider them truly foundational to the Gospel.

Perhaps the real key to understanding Wesley's attitude toward orthodoxy is his conviction that genuine religion is a matter of the heart. That is to say, it consists of a thorough moral and spiritual transformation. Such transformation, however, does not automatically accompany right belief. As Wesley put it:

> For neither does religion consist in orthodoxy or right opinions; which, although they are not properly outward things, are not in the heart, but the understanding. A man may be orthodox in every point; he may not only espouse right opinions, but zealously defend them against all opposers; he may think justly concerning the incarnation of our Lord, concerning the ever blessed Trinity, and every other doctrine contained in the oracles of God. . . . He may be almost as orthodox—as the devil . . . and may, all the while, be as great a stranger as he to the religion of the heart.[7]

As this passage indicates, Wesley's main reason for denying that orthodoxy is the essence of religion was because it is so easy to assume that if one's beliefs are in order, then so is his relationship with God. Because this is so, orthodoxy can be a very subtle substitute for real Christianity. As Wesley warned elsewhere: "And least of all dream that orthodoxy, right opinion, (vulgarly called *faith*), is religion. Of all religious dreams, this is the vainest; which takes hay and stubble for gold tried in the fire."[8]

The other side of this coin is Wesley's attitude toward

heresy. Though less well known than his comments on orthodoxy, his comments on heresy are equally reveal-ing. Consider, for instance, his note on Titus 3:10, which contains the Greek word *hairetikos* from which we derive the word heretic.

> This is the only place in the whole Scripture where this word *heretic* occurs; and here it evidently means a man that obstinately persists in contending about foolish questions, and thereby occasions strifes and animosities, schisms and parties in the Church. This, and this alone, is a *heretic* in the Scripture sense. . . . As for the popish sense, "A man that errs in fundamentals," although it crept, with many other things, early into the Church, yet it has no shadow of foundation, either in the Old or New Testaments.[9]

In Wesley's view, then, the term heretic has been traditionally used in a way which distorts its original Scriptual meaning.

Indeed, Wesley suggests that the label of heretic has often been used by "rich and honorable Christians" to stigmatize the "few that worshipped [God] in spirit and in truth."[10] Not surprisingly, Wesley defends such heretics while criticizing the champions of orthodoxy who opposed them. Thus, he defends Servetus against Calvin, Pelagius against Augustine, and Montanus against his second century critics. Wesley was even inclined to wonder "whether that arch-heretic, Montanus, was not one of the holiest men in the second century."[11]

It is important to realize that Wesley defended these so-called "heretics" because he believed their views had been misunderstood or misrepresented. (Wesley would be particularly sensitive to such misunderstanding because his own views were often distorted by critics who wanted to pin him with the charge of heresy!) He did not think that Servetus had denied the Trinity, nor that

Pelagius had denied the need for grace.

Whether or not he is correct in his interpretation of these men is not my concern here. What I do want to emphasize, however, is that in Wesley's view, just as the impeccably orthodox may lack real religion, so may the "heretics" have it. There is no simple correlation between real religion and right belief.

Wesley on the Value of Right Belief

It would be easy to conclude from all this that Wesley saw no real value in right belief. This conclusion, however, is quite premature. What then is his view of the role of right belief in the Christian life?

As we noted above, Wesley's critics forced him to clarify his claim that "orthodoxy, or right opinions, is, at best, but a very slender part of religion, if it can be allowed to be any part of it at all." Wesley's own explanation of this remark, I think, is a good gauge for determining his understanding of the part which right belief plays in real religion.

One of Wesley's critics, the Bishop of Gloucester, wrote a tract in which he charged Wesley with separating reason from grace and discarding reason from the service of religion. Part of the bishop's evidence for this charge was Wesley's remark about orthodoxy. The bishop's point was that orthodoxy is the rational aspect of religion.

In response, Wesley insisted that he constantly used reason "to distinguish between right and wrong opinions." And while he did not retract his controversial claim, he gave it a significant preface in the following:

After premising that it is our bounden duty to labour after a right judgment in all things, as a wrong judgment naturally leads to wrong practice, I say again, right opinion is at best but a slender part of religion (which properly and directly consists in

right tempers, words, and actions) and frequently it
is no part of religion.[12]

The principle that Wesley affirms here is surely a strong
one, namely, "that it is our bounden duty to labour after a
right judgment in all things." When right judgment is
conceived of as a duty, it is no longer in the realm of the
merely rational; rather, it is in the realm of the moral and
ethical.

Particularly important to notice here is *why* Wesley
thought it our duty to labor after right judgment,
namely, because there is a natural connection between
judgment and practice. Thus, right judgment is important, not as an end in itself but as a means to right
practice. The same thought is suggested when Wesley
says religion "directly" consists in right tempers, words,
and actions. The implication is that right opinion is an
indirect part of religion, insofar as right opinion leads to
right tempers, words, and actions. Or as Wesley
remarked later in his response to the bishop, "right
opinions are a great help, and wrong opinions a great
hindrance, to religion."[13]

A few years later, in his answer to another critic, Dr.
Erskine, Wesley affirmed an even stronger position on
the importance of right opinions. Erskine had written
that "right tempers cannot subsist without right opinion:
The love of God, for instance, cannot subsist without a
right opinion of Him." Wesley responded as follows.

I never said anything to the contrary: But this is
another question. Though right tempers cannot
subsist without right opinion, yet right opinion may
subsist without right tempers.[14]

Here Wesley is apparently granting that right opinion is
necessary to real religion, though its role is still an
indirect one.

Another substantial piece of evidence which shows

that Wesley emphasized the importance of right belief is in his definition of saving faith. Wesley recorded his understanding of saving faith in his *Journal* in response, again, to Dr. Erskine. After considering Erskine's account of saving faith, Wesley informs us, he found little to disagree with.

> I do not quarrel with the definition of faith in general—"a supernatural assent to the Word of God;" though I think "a supernatural conviction of the truths contained in the Word of God" is clearer. I allow, too, that the Holy Spirit enables us to perceive a peculiar light and glory in the Word of God, and particularly in the Gospel method of salvation: But I doubt whether saving faith be, properly, an assent to this light and glory. Is it not rather an assent (if we retain the word) to *the truths which God has revealed;* or more particularly, a divine conviction that "God was in Christ, reconciling the world unto Himself"?[15]

The point for emphasis here is that saving faith has a cognitive or propositional element. This is evident from the fact that Wesley defines faith as a conviction of the truths revealed in the Word of God. The truths about salvation are especially important, particularly those truths concerning Christ's saving work.

In his sermons, Wesley often enlarges on the meaning of saving faith in Christ. Wesley is always anxious to stress the personal dimension of faith. That is to say, saving faith believes that God loves *me,* that Christ died for *my* sins, and so on. But it is also clear that saving faith has a certain doctrinal content built into it. For instance, saving faith in Christ "acknowledges His death as the only sufficient means of redeeming man from death eternal, and His resurrection as the restoration of us all to life and immortality."[16]

Before closing this section, I want to look briefly at Wesley's sermon "On the Trinity." This short sermon is interesting because it exemplifies his outlook on the importance of doctrine and right belief. The sermon deals with a doctrine which is central to the Christian faith and was written relatively late in Wesley's career (1775), so it represents his mature thought.

He begins with his familiar point that religion is not right opinion and goes on to affirm that some truths are more important than others. These truths are of "deep importance." One such truth, according to Wesley, is that God is Three in One.

While Wesley insists on the importance of believing this truth, he is equally concerned to maintain that it is not necessary to believe any particular explication of it. Detailed elaborations of the doctrine are a matter of opinion, not of essential belief. Wesley himself thinks the Athanasian Creed is the best explication of the Trinity, but he would not require others to assent to it. He insists only that the substance of the doctrine must be believed, and he allows that that substance may be expressed in different ways. Indeed, Wesley would not insist that anyone use the word Trinity. He would insist only on the bare words of Scripture which pertain to the Trinity.

Why, then, does Wesley think it essential to believe in the Trinity? In his words: "It [the doctrine of the Trinity] enters into the very heart of Christianity: It lies at the root of all vital religion. Unless these Three are One, how can all men honour the Son, even as they honour the Father?"[17] In other words, proper worship is at the heart of vital religion, and proper worship of God requires that the Son of God receive equal honor with the Father. Furthermore, such worship is appropriate only if the Father and the Son are One.

Moreover, the very experience of knowing that one is a child of God is Trinitarian. One cannot even be a Christian believer "till God the Holy Ghost witnesses that God the Father has accepted him through the merits of God the Son: and having this witness, he honours the Son, and the blessed Spirit, 'even as he honours the

Father.' "[18] Such Christian belief is the dynamic of that vital religion which results in right actions, tempers, and words. Because the truth that God is Three in One is so integral to the Christian life, Wesley does not see how anyone who denies this doctrine can be saved.

To conclude this section, we may summarize Wesley's view of the importance of right belief as follows. First, right belief is an indirect component of right action and right worship. Second, a certain doctrinal content is inherent in saving faith. Although it is not necessary to use traditional theological expressions in affirming the faith, it is essential to believe the substance of the central Christian truths in order to enjoy a saving relationship with God.

Wesley on Catholic Spirit

Let us turn now to examine Wesley's famous sermon, "Catholic Spirit." I want to determine whether the definition in our *Discipline's* glossary is an accurate account of Wesley's notion of catholic spirit. I also want to consider the claim that the theological spectrum in United Methodism can be justified by appeal to catholic spirit.

In the first place, it is important to realize that an emphasis on love pervades this sermon. Wesley begins by observing that, according to Scripture, love is due to all mankind, especially to those who love God. And at the end of the sermon Wesley comes back to stress the importance of love for all mankind: "And he that has this is of a catholic spirit. For love alone gives the title to this character: Catholic love is a catholic spirit."[19]

Wesley's concern is that theological and ecclesiastical differences often prevent this kind of love within the Christian community, where it should be most evident. As he puts it, Christians cannot all think alike, and consequently they cannot all walk alike. This is another instance of his general point that opinion affects practice.

It is in the face of this reality that Wesley holds up the ideal of catholic spirit.

> But although a difference of opinions or modes of worship may prevent an entire external union; yet need it prevent our union in affection? Though we cannot think alike, may we not love alike? May we not be of one heart, though we are not of one opinion?[20]

We noted above that it is not always clear what Wesley means by opinion. In this sermon, he does not give us any examples of opinions which divide the Christian community. However, he does specify some of the different modes of worship which prevent external union. Included under this head are different forms of church government, different forms of prayer, and different modes of administering the sacraments. While these differences are not strictly matters of opinion, they spring from differences of opinion.

Particularly interesting are the reasons Wesley gives for tolerance on these "smaller points" of difference. In the first place, he cites the limitations of human understanding. "It is an unavoidable consequence of the present weakness and shortness of human understanding, that several men will be of several minds in religion as well as in common life." Furthermore, "no man can be assured that all his own opinions, taken together, are true. Nay, every thinking man is assured they are not."[21] Thus, Wesley accounts for religious differences in terms of the weakness of human understanding, and he calls for tolerance on the ground that none of us can be sure all our opinions are true.

A second reason for tolerance is that everyone must follow his own conscience. "God has given no right to any of the children of men . . . to lord it over the conscience of his brethren; but every man must judge for himself, as every man must give an account of himself to God." This principle is especially significant for Wesley, for in his view, it is this "right of private judgment on which the whole Reformation stands."[22]

A third reason given by Wesley is that one's opinions are not a matter of choice: "I can no more think, than I can see or hear, as I will."[23] This argument is especially interesting. Wesley's view is that we are generally passive with respect to our beliefs. That is, we do not choose our beliefs any more than we choose to see whatever we generally see.

Thus, with respect to sight, we just automatically receive stimulation from whatever is in our visual field and find ourselves seeing whatever is there. For example, if a tree is in our visual field, we do not choose to see it, we just see it. In the same way, Wesley is suggesting, our opinions reflect the way we "see" things. We do not choose our opinions in any straightforward way, and we should not be expected simply to change them at will.[24]

The upshot of all this is that Christians have good reasons to be tolerant of one another with respect to "smaller points" of difference. The limitation of our understanding and the recognition that some of our opinions will surely turn out to be wrong give plenty of warrant for modesty and humility when dealing with points of difference. The responsibility of every person to follow his own conscience means that no one can set up his conscience to be another person's guide, particularly since opinions are not simply a matter of choice. If these arguments are sound, "smaller points" of difference should provide no barrier to catholic spirit.

And yet, somewhat surprisingly, Wesley goes on to emphasize in very strong language that catholic spirit does not mean taking a casual attitude toward matters of opinion.

It is not an indifference to all opinions: This is the spawn of hell, not the offspring of heaven. This

> unsettledness of thought, this being "driven to and
> fro, and tossed about with every wind of doctrine," is
> a great curse, not a blessing; an irreconcilable
> enemy, not a friend, to true catholicism.[25]

Apparently, Wesley thought it important to have settled
views, even on matters of opinion which are not essential
doctrine. As we noted above, he was himself a man of
strong views, so he exemplified this principle very well.
His only concern was that differences of opinion should
not stand in the way of Christian love and cooperation.

If it is important to have settled views on matters of
opinion, it is even more vital to have solid convictions on
essential doctrine.

> A man of truly catholic spirit, has not now his
> religion to seek. He is fixed as the sun in his
> judgment concerning the main branches of Chris-
> tian doctrine.[26]

Clearly, some doctrines are altogether non-negotiable
for "a man of truly catholic spirit."

Earlier in his sermon, Wesley mentions some of the
doctrines which a person of catholic spirit will believe.
These have to do primarily with the nature of God and
the nature of Christ. More specifically, Wesley cites such
divine "perfections" as eternity, wisdom, justice, and
sovereignty. For Wesley, believing such things is a deeply
spiritual matter. He assumes that having a heart right
with God involves certain beliefs.

With respect to Christ, it is noteworthy that Wesley
applies the description "God over all, blessed forever,"
which he clearly takes to be an affirmation of Christ's
deity.[27] Indeed, the deity of Christ is one doctrine which
Wesley emphasized many times in his writings. He felt it
was necessary to be explicit on this point, even if some
found the doctrine distasteful. As he put it, "on this I
must insist, as the foundation of all our hope."[28] He was

fully prepared to "think and let think" on "all opinions which do not strike at the root of Christianity." But in Wesley's view, to deny that Christ is "the eternal, supreme God" would strike at the root.[29]

It is worth noting that Wesley gave a more detailed statement of basic doctrine in another essay which is very similar in spirit to his sermon on catholic spirit, namely, his "A Letter to a Roman Catholic." As Albert Outler remarks, this letter "is consistent with Wesley's familiar distinction between essential beliefs and heterogenous opinions; it is also a fair sample of what he actually meant by 'catholic spirit.' "[30]

Not surprisingly, Wesley's statement of essential beliefs in this letter is composed primarily of an exposition of the doctrines set forth in the early creeds. He mentions such points as the existence of God, creation, and God's sovereignty over creation; the deity of Christ, and His death, resurrection, and ascension; the deity of the Holy Spirit, the founding of the Church by Christ, the forgiveness of sins, and the final judgment. Moreover, Wesley includes in his list those doctrines which modern churchmen choke on most easily: angels, the miraculous conception of Christ, bodily resurrection, and hell.[31] Indeed, this list provides ample support for Outler's observation that: "Wesley is quite specific and quite adamant about the essential doctrines of Christianity—and quite 'orthodox'!"[32]

Now, it might be objected that Wesley's arguments for tolerance on "smaller points" should also apply to doctrines such as the deity of Christ. For instance, what if someone appealed to Wesley's argument that one's opinions are not a matter of choice and simply insisted that, in his view, Christ was not God? What would Wesley say to this? Consider the following.

> I really think, that if an hundred, or an hundred thousand, sincere, honest (I add, humble, modest, self-diffident) men were, with attention and care, to

> read over the New Testament, uninfluenced by any
> but the Holy Spirit, nine in ten of them, at least, if
> not every one, would discover that the Son of God
> was "adorable," and one God with the Father; and
> would be immediately led to "honour Him, even as
> they honoured the Father."[33]

This suggests that Wesley would be inclined to think that anyone who denied the deity of Christ either had not investigated the matter carefully enough or was not sufficiently honest. Apparently Wesley thought the main branches of Christian doctrine had been revealed so clearly in Scripture that virtually no one would have good reason to deny them.

Catholic Spirit and Contemporary Pluralism

Let us turn now to the question of whether the definition of doctrinal pluralism from the glossary of our *Discipline* is, as it purports to be, a faithful summary of Wesley's sermon on catholic spirit. As explained in the previous chapter, the *Discipline's* definition accounts for theological diversity by appealing to the limitations of language for expressing truth. Since language is limited in this way, different verbal expressions may state the same truth in complementary fashion. Thus, such theological diversity is primarily verbal in nature, rather than substantial. Moreover, this principle applies to essential theological doctrines as well as to secondary issues.

In the light of our analysis of Wesley's sermon, I am afraid we must conclude that the *Discipline's* definition is not an accurate account of catholic spirit. In the first place, different reasons are given to account for theological diversity. Wesley's appeal, remember, was not to the limitations of language but to the limitations of human understanding. While there is a relation between the limitations of language and the limitations of human understanding, they are not the same. Furthermore, Wesley's primary aim was not to account for theological differences but to argue for tolerance on smaller points of difference.

This is not to say that Wesley would disagree with the main thrust of our *Discipline's* definition. For he recognized the limitations of language and allowed that the same truth could be expressed in more than one way. Indeed, he argued that, in many cases, theological controversies are at bottom primarily a matter of different parties using different words, language, and modes of expression.[34] However, this is not his point in "Catholic Spirit."

Thus, a second important difference between our *Discipline's* definition and Wesley's sermon concerns the nature of theological diversity. In our *Discipline's* definition, theological differences are primarily verbal in nature, while in Wesley, the differences in question are not merely verbal but substantial. For instance, some baptize infants while others baptize only mature believers. For Wesley, one of these positions is correct and the other is wrong. Both positions cannot be right, as they might be if the difference was only verbal. Wesley is not concerned to dissolve the difference but only to argue that it is a minor point and the parties involved can still love and cooperate with each other. Furthermore, whereas Wesley is concerned in "Catholic Spirit" only with smaller points of difference, the principle in our *Discipline's* definition applies to major doctrines as well, as we have already noted.

In short, while the main thrust of the *Discipline's* definition accords with Wesley's overall thought, it is not a faithful summary of Wesley's sermon on catholic spirit.

Now, what about the *Discipline's* claim that the contemporary theological scene exemplifies Wesley's ideal of catholic spirit? I think the answer to this question is apparent. The contemporary scene is not a model of Wesley's catholic spirit for the simple reason that the theological spectrum of today goes far beyond the limits Wesley insisted upon. The contemporary scene does not display agreement on such matters as the nature of God and the deity of Christ. These matters are considered to be as negotiable as anything else in contemporary theology.

Concluding Remarks

In the previous chapter, I pointed out that our *Discipline* confuses at least two distinct understandings of theological pluralism. In view of our discussion in this chapter, we must now conclude that a third understanding of pluralism is involved in the confusion. For while theological pluralism is identified with Wesley's catholic spirit, we have seen that neither of the two understandings of pluralism we distinguished in the previous chapter are true to his understanding of that notion.

Indeed, the whole attempt in our Doctrinal Statement to bolster contemporary theological pluralism with Wesleyan legitimacy strikes me as strained and awkward at best. At worst, it is an example of the concept of catholic spirit dangerously applied, against which Wesley wisely warned.

A judicious application of Wesley's catholic spirit, however, would be healthy for the entire Wesleyan tradition. Conservative Wesleyan denominations should learn from it to be more tolerant and flexible with respect to doctrines which are not truly essential to the faith. Such groups often betray their Wesleyan roots by displaying a narrow party view. United Methodists, on the other hand, need to learn from Wesley that some doctrines really are essential and that these define the limits of tolerance.

4

A PROBLEM OF COHERENCE

One of the often-observed ironies is that those who profess to be inclusive and open to all viewpoints are often remarkably intolerant. This observation is relevant to our subject because one understanding of pluralism which we have discussed demands complete openness. This notion of pluralism is expressed in the following passage.

> All claims to Christian truth deserve an open and fair hearing for their sifting and assessment. The viability of all doctrinal opinion demands that the processes of theological development must be kept open-ended, both on principle and in fact (p. 83)

Those who adhere to such principles should be genuinely open to all claims to Christian truth.

In fact, however, those who profess to be committed to pluralism sometimes betray their profession in some unlikely ways. Ira Gallaway pointed to this phenomenon in his discussion of "The Confusion of Pluralism":

I have found that many of the leaders of modern secular liberalism do not hesitate to go to the theological jugular vein of anyone who with some cogency and success advances the evangelical or orthodox theological understanding of the Christian faith to which I am committed. This is inevitably done by branding such a person as a "fundamentalist," a "reactionary," or as one who is either ignorant or does not think. As I have indicated before, this seems to me to be a fundamentalism of liberalism that is just as judgmental and exclusivistic as any reactionary fundamentalism of the past or present. . . . This liberalism is peculiarly illiberal in attitude and practice.[1]

Gallaway has had a great deal of experience serving the church in a variety of capacities, so his charge must be taken seriously.

However, perhaps it is worthwhile to cite one more witness of this phenomenon. Richard G. Hutcheson, Jr. has also had broad experience in mainline churches, having served as a denominational executive in the Presbyterian Church. Hutcheson describes himself as one with a liberal background, whose every instinct is to "respond to situations in liberal ways." So it is particularly interesting when he goes on to record the following opinion.

Yet after six years of close, intensive observation in the heart of one mainline denominational bureaucracy, and with continual opportunities to observe others, I have come to the reluctant conclusion that the evangelical perception is, on the whole, accurate. Mainline establishments are wide open to cultural pluralism, but not to liberal evangelical pluralism. Out of the highest of motives—response to what they are convinced is God's claim on the Church—they are manipulating every possible organizational,

political, and budgetary process to maintain one
unified model of church life and mission.[2]

As Hutcheson's quote indicates, this liberal exclusiveness
has large practical implications. That is, the practical
upshot is that evangelicals and others of traditional
mindset are excluded, as much as possible, from
policy-making. Though every attempt may be made to
assure significant input from racial and cultural minorities, evangelicals are often consciously prevented from
exercising real influence.

How is this peculiar phenomenon of liberal exclusiveness to be explained? Is this just a curious side-effect of
the policy of pluralism which can, and should, be
eliminated? Or is this ironic exclusiveness actually
intrinsic to the notion of pluralism?

Discovering Incoherence

Let us proceed—with these questions in mind—by
spelling out explicitly what I will call the principles of
pluralism.

1) All claims to Christian truth deserve an open
   and fair hearing for sifting and assessment.
2) All doctrinal opinion is viable.
3) The processes of theological development must
   be kept completely open-ended.
4) No claim to Christian truth is welcome which is
   "intolerant or exclusive" toward other serious
   theological opinions (cf. *Discipline,* p. 82).

Now let us raise a question. Suppose someone were to put
forth the claim that the principles of pluralism are
inimical to Christian truth. Should this claim be given a
fair hearing and a serious assessment?

A little reflection suggests that this question poses
something of a dilemma. For on the one hand if, like all

other claims to Christian truth, the principles of pluralism are open to assessment, then it is at least possible that they could be shown to be inimical to Christian truth. And if this were shown, then presumably the principles of pluralism should be rejected. If, on the other hand, the principles of pluralism claim to be above assessment, then they assume a position which they deny to other theological claims. This surely seems inconsistent.

Indeed, this line of thinking raises serious questions about the very coherence of the principles of pluralism. In his discussion of the "conditions for coherence" Richard Swinburne explains what makes a statement incoherent: "Clearly if a statement P entails a self-contradictory statement, then P is incoherent—for it has buried in it a claim that something is so and that it is not so—and it is not conceivable that things should be thus."[3] Elsewhere he states: "All self-contradictory statements are of course incoherent. But many incoherent statements are not straightforwardly self-contradictory."[4]

Thus, if an incoherent statement is not straightforwardly self-contradictory, it can be shown to be self-contradictory by drawing out its implications. That is, the statement will entail other statements which produce a contradiction. It is my opinion that the principles of pluralism are incoherent precisely in this manner—they are self-contradictory, but not straightforwardly so.

In order to show this, let us apply the principles of pluralism to one important example of a claim to Christian truth which clearly falls within the doctrinal guidelines of the United Methodist Church, namely, traditional orthodox theology. Notice the tension which results when the claims of traditional theology are spelled out in relation to the principles of pluralism.

5) Traditional theology denies that all doctrinal opinion is viable (e.g., doctrinal opinion which

interprets the Incarnation in any way which denies the essential oneness of Christ with the Father, His pre-existence, miraculous conception, or bodily resurrection).

6) Traditional theology holds that the main branches of Christian doctrine are "as fixed as the sun," (Wesley) so that the processes of theological development cannot be kept completely open-ended.

Now then, with these counter claims before us, we can easily see how to draw out the incoherence which lies buried in the principles of pluralism.

7) The principles of pluralism and traditional theology make claims which are mutually exclusive.

If a pair of claims are mutually exclusive, to affirm one of the claims is to reject the other. And if one clearly rejects a claim, presumably he means to deny its viability. If this is so, it is apparent that:

8) To affirm the principles of pluralism is to deny the viability of at least one serious claim to Christian truth.

9) But to deny the viability of any serious claim to Christian truth is to violate the principles of pluralism.

Thus, in order to remain faithful to the principles of pluralism, it seems that one must be prepared to affirm both of the following.

10) The claims of traditional theology are viable.

11) The claims of traditional theology are not viable.

Since the principles of pluralism lead to a contradiction, we must conclude:

12) Therefore, the principles of pluralism are incoherent.

The Way Out

The question may arise of whether traditional theology is the only example of a Christian truth claim which cannot be absolutely denied or affirmed without rendering the principles of pluralism incoherent. If we think about this for a moment, it seems apparent that any truth claim which excludes contrary truth claims will bring the same result. Anyone who insists on any truth claim at all cannot embrace the principles of pluralism without thereby calling his own truth claim into question.

Apparently then, the principles of pluralism are compatible with only one kind of a truth claim, and that is a tentative one. If all truth claims are tentative, then even contradictory claims can exist with some measure of consistency; for a tentative claim is, by definition, very much open to the possibility of being wrong. If all claims to Christian truth are viable, but none are clearly right or wrong, then the principles of pluralism are quite plausible. Something like this is involved in the following.

> . . . our awareness of the transcendent mystery of divine truth allows us in good conscience to acknowledge the positive virtues of doctrinal pluralism even within the same community of believers, not merely because such an attitude is realistic (p. 73).

The suggestion here, I think, is that divine truth is too mysterious to allow any definite knowledge of it. And if no one has any definite knowledge of divine truth, it would be presumptuous to rule out any doctrinal opinion. There simply are no criteria for such judgments.

Now, if this is an accurate account of divine truth, it is good news for the advocates of pluralism. The bad news, however, is that all doctrinal affirmations are thereby reduced to the status of conjecture.

This obviously runs against the grain of the kind of hearty belief which has characterized the Christian faith. Of course, a large element of mystery has always been recognized in the Christian tradition. Our knowledge of God is not exhaustive, nor can it be proven to everyone who questions it. Nevertheless, the conviction of believers through the centuries has been that we do have substantial knowledge of divine truth.

So the question persists whether any theological claims should be affirmed as clearly true or whether all such affirmations must be merely hypothetical or conjectural, as the principles of pluralism seem to entail. If the advocates of pluralism accept the conclusion that all theological truth claims are conjectural, their consistency problem remains. For the claim that "all theological truth claims are conjectural" is itself a theological truth claim, and a very far reaching one at that.[5]

What are the warrants for this claim? Is it self-evident to reason or intuitively obvious? Is it a revelation from God? Apparently it is none of these. But even more to the point, is it true or merely a guess that all theological truth claims must be conjectural? If it is held to be *true*, then it must be admitted that *not all* theological truth claims have to be *conjectural*. On the other hand, if it is mere speculation, why should we yield to it? Either way, we cannot coherently maintain that all theological truth claims must be conjectural or tentative.

It is important to stress here that the principles of pluralism are incoherent precisely because they represent an exclusive position which (inconsistently) denies the right of any theological position to be exclusive toward other serious opinions. The principles of pluralism are set up as the judge of all theological claims, and exclude as unacceptable any which dare to claim more than a tentative status.

The force of this must be clearly seen. Pluralism masquerades as tolerance. It appears to guarantee fairness and equal treatment for all serious opinions. The problem, to reiterate, is that some serious views claim more than a tentative status and are therefore exclusive in a way which puts a definite stricture on pluralism. In such cases, it is impossible to recognize the validity of both the exclusive claim and the views which it excludes. A standoff is inevitable, and the advocate of pluralism must side against all exclusive claims which are not content to accept a tentative status.

It appears, then, that the only way to be consistent is frankly to admit that some truth claims are basic, normative, and non-negotiable. If this is recognized from the outset, there is no inconsistency in denying that all doctrinal opinion is viable. On the other hand, to hold that all doctrinal opinion is viable, as the advocates of pluralism must, is to land immediately in contradiction.

Conclusion

By now we should not find so surprising the peculiar phenomenon of liberal exclusiveness. Because the principles of pluralism are clearly exclusive, those who profess commitment to them will inevitably be intolerant of theological positions, such as traditional orthodoxy, which make claims to absolute or final truth. The examples of exclusiveness which we noted at the beginning of this chapter simply illustrate, I suspect, the practical outworking of the actual logic of pluralism.

As George Lindbeck has pointed out, those who profess to be creedless are not genuinely creedless.

"When creedlessness is insisted on as a mark of group identity, it becomes by definition operationally creedal."[6] So perhaps in reality the principles of pluralism have come to function as a creed in our church. Surely this is ironic, if not incoherent.

5

PLURALISM AND THE PROBLEM OF AUTHORITY

In the previous chapter, I argued that some doctrinal truth claims should be frankly identified as normative and non-negotiable. To say this is to raise the whole question of authority. What warrants can be given for taking any truth claim as normative?

Contemporary theology is marked by a crisis of authority. Ironically, however, when authority breaks down, claims to authority increase rather than decrease. So there is today no shortage of theological pronouncements coming from every quarter. The contemporary scene can be aptly described as a cacophony of voices vying for attention and allegiance. Given so many competing viewpoints, the question of authority is inevitable. To raise the question, unfortunately, does not guarantee an answer. Instead, one may be forced to the unhappy conclusion that much contemporary theology has simply bypassed the authority question.

To some observers, theology no longer seems like a discipline. Rather, as Paul Holmer has remarked, theology too often "looks like free creation." The connection between theology as "free creation" and the loss of authority is evident. As Holmer goes on to say: "Where everything counts as theology, we can safely say that scarcely anything really counts. Clearly, we have become uncertain of the criteria or even whether there are any at all."[1]

It is obvious then, that if theology is to be taken seriously, the question of authority must be addressed. Those who put forth theological claims and proposals cannot evade the issue of criteria for truth. Rather, such persons should forthrightly identify their criteria and the warrants for them.

A Wesleyan Solution

The issue of authority is particularly relevant to the United Methodist Church, with its affirmation of theological pluralism. The question is, what understanding of authority could license open-ended pluralism? Or does the presence of such pluralism indicate that there is no authority for United Methodist theology?

Our Doctrinal Statement is sensitive to this issue and, in fact, provides an answer in the section headed "Doctrinal Guidelines in the United Methodist Church." The section begins by posing the question of how our doctrinal reflection and construction can be "most fruitful and fulfilling," given that established doctrinal standards "are not to be construed literally and juridically."

The answer comes in terms of our free inquiry within the boundaries defined by four main sources and guidelines for Christian theology: Scripture, tradition, experience, reason. These four are interdependent; none can be defined unambiguously. They allow for, indeed they positively encourage, variety in United Methodist theologizing. Jointly, they have provided a broad and stable context for reflection and formulation (p.78).

So the United Methodist solution to the authority problem is to be found in what has come to be known as the "Wesleyan Quadrilateral," namely Scripture, tradition, reason, and experience.[2] In the place of traditional doctrinal standards, then, we have guidelines which provide only a "context" for theological reflection and formulation. Thus, we have an understanding of authority which not only allows for, but positively encourages theological pluralism.

This is certainly an interesting proposal which deserves careful consideration. It has considerable merit because it does not rest the entire weight of authority on a single, isolated norm. Rather, it recognizes that the authority of Scripture interacts in a complex fashion with tradition, reason, and experience.

However, the proposal also raises a number of important questions. A preliminary concern has to do with the connection between Wesley and the quadrilateral. The connection is not quite as simple as the phrase "Wesleyan Quadrilateral" might suggest. For while Wesley did appeal to each of the four elements of the quadrilateral to defend his theology, it is not at all apparent that he would agree that the quadrilateral allows for the kind of theological variety which characterizes United Methodism today. The phrase is also misleading if it is taken to mean that Wesley viewed all four elements of the quadrilateral as equal in authority, for he clearly took Scripture as the first and final authority in theological disputes.[3] Furthermore, the definitions of the four criteria which appear in our Doctrinal Statement seem to be shaped more by modern understandings than by Wesley.

However, my main concern in this chapter is not whether our Statement is faithful to Wesley in its presentation of the quadrilateral. This is not a major issue, as our Doctrinal Statement does not explicitly claim to be following Wesley with respect to the quadrilateral.

The question I do want to pursue is whether the quadrilateral can provide us with an adequate account of authority. I particularly want to examine what our Statement says about the authority of Scripture and its relation to the other three criteria. In other words, I want to consider in what sense the authority of Scripture is "interdependent" with the other elements of the quadrilateral. While I will make significant use of Wesley, my aim is not merely to interpret Wesley but to offer a positive account of authority which does justice to the quadrilateral.

This will inevitably involve a number of controversial issues which I cannot fully explore. What follows is no more than a sketch of what would be required in a full blown account of authority. But given the importance of the connection between authority and the problem of pluralism, I think it is essential at least to lay bare the main contours of such an account.

Experience: Basic but Subordinate

It has been generally agreed, at least in principle, that Scripture is a higher authority than the other three criteria in the quadrilateral. As our Doctrinal Statement puts it: "United Methodists share with all other Christians the conviction that Scripture is the primary source and guideline for doctrine" (p. 78). The unique authority of Scripture has been especially emphasized among Protestant Christians. *Sola Scriptura* (Scripture alone) was a Reformation motto which expressed the conviction that Scripture is the only infallible source of authority in the church, and that other sources must be subordinate to it.

It may seem puzzling, at least initially, that Scripture can be thought superior in authority to the other three criteria as well as interdependent with them. For if Scripture is a higher authority than the other elements of the quadrilateral, how can it in any sense depend upon them?

In order to answer this question, let us begin to reflect on what it means to accept the authority of Scripture. As a working formulation, I would suggest the following: To accept the authority of Scripture is to believe that Scripture gives us an accurate account of how God has revealed Himself, His will, and His purposes. It is to believe that the events recorded in Scripture, which purport to tell us how God has revealed Himself, actually happened. These have to do primarily with God's saving acts in Israel and in Jesus Christ. To accept the authority of Scripture is to accept, furthermore, the interpretations of God's saving acts which were given by prophets and apostles, including moral and practical directives.

Notice that believing all this involves another important assumption, namely, that the people of Biblical times had certain experiences. The Old Testament people of God experienced deliverance from captivity in Egypt; some witnessed the plagues and the crossing of the Red Sea; others took part in the conquest of Canaan, and so on. Similarly in New Testament times, some witnessed the ministry of Jesus, including His miracles, and some were fortunate enough to see Him after His resurrection and to witness His ascension. Throughout the entire period of Biblical revelation, there were prophets and apostles who experienced God speaking to them and inspiring them to communicate His will to His people.

What this points up, clearly enough, is that appeal to the authority of Scripture logically involves a more basic appeal to *experience,* namely, to the experience of the Biblical writers.[4] It is because we have become convinced that the Biblical writers had certain experiences that we appeal to the authority of Scripture. Or, in other words, we do not believe the events recorded in Scripture occurred simply because they are recorded in Scripture so much as we believe Scripture because we have become convinced that these events occurred and that God has revealed Himself through them.

The further question may naturally arise as to why we believe God has revealed Himself through the events recorded in Scripture. Why are the Scriptures authoritative for us rather than, say, the Koran? These are questions which go to the very foundation of the debate about the rationality and justification of religious belief. While it is important to deal with such questions in any complete account of religious rationality, we cannot pursue them here.[5]

But let us come back to the question of whether it is consistent to hold that Scripture is a higher authority than experience, if appeal to Scripture involves a logically prior appeal to experience. In response to this difficulty, William J. Abraham has suggested that we need to distinguish between the question of canon in theology and the question of the foundations of our knowledge, including knowledge of God. Or in other words, we must distinguish between the question of theological norms and questions of fundamental epistemology. Thus, while Scripture is a higher authority than experience in the realm of theological norms, experience has logical precedence in the realm of fundamental epistemology.

Abraham offers an analogy to explain this point, which I paraphrase as follows. Suppose I am fortunate enough to have a close, personal relationship with the president of the United States. Suppose further that the president reveals certain things to me, and that later I include this material in a book. What the president revealed to me was mediated through the senses. I did not come to know it from innate ideas or by inferring it from his public actions. But what I write may become normative in the sense that it is relied upon to give an accurate account of the president. And furthermore, you may come to know the president and your experience may confirm what I have written about him.

Abraham goes on to make explicit the lessons of his analogy.

> Likewise, certain people may have access through their experience to those special acts of God in the past which uniquely make known what God is like. Because of their unique position, their reflection has a privileged position as normative. Yet their reflection depends crucially . . . on their experience. What they know is not given to them through innate ideas or intuition, nor is it inferred in any straightforward sense from nature or history.[6]

Thus it is that Scripture occupies a place of unique authority. For it "embodies special revelation given in the past to the people of God."[7] The claim that such past revelation is normative for our time assumes, of course, that the canon of authoritative Scripture is closed.[8]

Our analogy also makes clear how experience functions in the realm of theological norms, namely, to confirm what Scripture teaches. Wesley agreed with the principle that "Experience is not sufficient to prove a doctrine which is not founded on Scripture." He insisted, however, that if a doctrine can be shown to be grounded in Scripture, then it is proper to appeal to experience to confirm that doctrine.[9] In the realm of theological norms, then, given a canon of Scripture, experience plays a much more modest role than it does at the level of basic epistemology.

In order to see more clearly why this is so, it is helpful to spell out more fully just what Wesley meant by spiritual experience. The key point is that he construed such experience as analogous to ordinary sense experience. Generally speaking, for Wesley, experience is, as

Rex Matthews put it, "what happens when something in the external world impinges on the senses."[10] This is true in both the natural realm and the spiritual realm. However, we can only experience God and the spiritual world if God has opened up the spiritual senses in our soul by an act of grace. We do not possess the necessary spiritual senses in our fallen condition, and we can only receive them if we are "born again."[11]

When our spiritual senses are thus restored, there is an objectivity about spiritual experience which parallels our experience of the natural world. Matthews draws the parallel as follows.

> For Wesley there is an immediacy and objectivity about the sensory experience of the external world: when you stub your toe on a rock, there is no doubt about the objectivity of your experience, nor about the reality of the rock . . . Just so, for Wesley there is an immediacy and objectivity about the experience of the external spiritual world through "the spiritual senses": when the Spirit "witnesses" to your spirit that Christ has died for your sins and that for His sake you are saved from the law of sin and death, you "know" that as objective fact, precisely as you "know" about the rock. In either case, experience provides objective evidence about the being and nature of that which is experienced, and knowledge is what results from the application of reason to that experiential evidence.[12]

The failure to grasp the objectivity of spiritual experience in Wesley's thought can easily lead to misunderstanding of his theology. It has been argued, for instance, that Wesley's emphasis on experience prepared the way for the classical liberal, experience-oriented theology of the nineteenth century. Wesley's objective view of experience, however, is quite at odds with the subjective understanding of experience which was central to liberal theology in the following centuries.[13]

It is because spiritual experience is objective in this sense that our experience may confirm the teaching of Scripture. That is, it is because we experience the same objective reality which the Biblical writers experienced that our experience can be expected to be consonant with what they have written of theirs.

Of course, some of the experiences of the Biblical writers were unique, and thus cannot be shared by modern believers. For instance, modern believers have not seen Christ in His resurrected body, as did the early disciples. Nevertheless, present day believers can fully share in Paul's experience of knowing that Christ is alive and lives in them (cf. Galatians 2:20). If our experience matches Paul's at this point, this also tends to confirm the rest of his teaching about Christ, even though much of what he wrote was based on his privileged position as an apostle. Going back to our analogy about the president: if your experience of the president matched certain elements of my account, you would be inclined to trust the rest of my account, even if you were not in a position personally to confirm it. Thus, while our experience may directly confirm significant portions of Biblical teaching, it can only indirectly confirm, at best, other portions.

But what if our experience does not confirm the teaching of Scripture? What if our experience does not fit the categories of Scripture or even clashes with Scripture? If genuine spiritual experience is indeed objective, as Wesley thought, the reasonable thing to conclude in such cases is that our experience is of a different reality than that experienced by the Biblical writers.

What we must *not* do, if Scripture is to remain normative for us, is use our experience to place limits on Biblical authority. In this light, consider the following.

The task of authentic Biblical hermeneutics is to aid

the Church in discerning the divine will. This will require labor at the intersection of the Biblical story with our story. What is authoritative in the Biblical witness must be consistent with what the Church knows from its experience with a living God.[14]

The principle laid down here is an unwarranted restriction of Biblical authority. For the Biblical witness may not be consistent with our experience due to the fact that our experience of God is impoverished or distorted. Moreover, how can we really be open to discern the divine will if we accept Biblical authority only to the extent that it fits our own limited experience of God? For God may be calling us to a level of experience that we have not known before.

A generation ago, Edwin Lewis of Drew University spoke a prophetic word to the Church of his day because it had substituted various liberal ideologies for historic Christianity. Lewis remarked: "How far have we gotten with our various substitutes? Look over our churches: they are full of people, who, brought up on these substitutes, are strangers to those deeper experiences without which there had been no New Testament and no Church of Christ."[15]

Lewis was writing during a period in which Methodist theology was based primarily in experience.[16] Ironically, when theology is based primarily in experience, genuine spiritual experience may actually be undermined. This is an important lesson for our own day, when appeal to experience often takes precedence over Scripture. If we are to recover a robust sense of Biblical authority, it is essential that we return experience to a subordinate role. While it can confirm Scriptural teaching, it cannot function as rival in the realm of theological norms. It is when experience plays this more modest role that vital spiritual experience, like that of the New Testament writers, can best flourish.

Divine Revelation and Human Perception

When it is recognized that appeal to the authority of Scripture involves a logically prior appeal to the experience of the people of Biblical times, including the Biblical writers, other problems must be faced. Most significantly, questions may be raised about the interpretation which the Biblical writers gave of their experience. It may even be doubted whether they really understood their experience.

Recall, for example, our earlier discussion of John Hick's view of the doctrine of the Incarnation. He thinks the doctrine was largely inspired by the early Christian experience of reconciliation with God. Those early disciples, according to Hick, were drawn into a life which "was pervaded by a glorious sense of the divine forgiveness and love." They easily associated their sense of forgiveness with Jesus' death because it was axiomatic for them, as Jews, that "without the shedding of blood there is no forgiveness" (Hebrews 9:22, NIV).

> There was thus a natural transition in their minds from the experience of reconciliation with God as Jesus' disciples, to the thought of his death as an atoning sacrifice, and from this to the conclusion that in order for Jesus' death to have been a sufficient atonement for human sin he must himself have been divine.[17]

It was this initial development in the early Christian experience, Hick thinks, which led ultimately to the Nicene doctrine which explicitly affirms that Christ was God the Son incarnate, of one substance with the Father.

Hick is sympathetic to orthodox Christianity in the sense that he thinks it was an effective way to express the significance of Jesus in the cultural milieu of that time. But now, however, Hick thinks it is time for Christians to "outgrow" the literal interpretation of the Incarnation and recognize traditional language about Christ as "the hyperbole of the heart."[18] So, in the end, Hick regards the traditional doctrines of the Incarnation, Atonement, and so on as mistakes to be rejected.

In short then, Hick thinks there was misunderstanding, natural though it was, at two important levels in the development of Christian doctrine. In the first place, the early disciples, including the Biblical writers, did not really understand the meaning of their experience of Jesus. They were overzealous in ascribing divinity to Him, and gave us at best a distorted picture of Him. Secondly, the Church perpetuated the misunderstanding of the early disciples and even took it a step farther when it formulated its official doctrine of Christ in the ecumenical creeds.

If we are to hold a substantial view of Biblical authority, I think it is essential that we reject both of these notions. That is, we must maintain that the Biblical writers gave us an accurate account of who Christ is and His significance for us.[19] Furthermore, we must insist that the early ecumenical creeds are true interpretations of the Biblical witness. This second claim is especially relevant for our purposes since it focuses, as I shall show, the manner in which the authority of Scripture is interdependent with the criteria of tradition and reason.

The first claim, however, is fundamental to the second. For there is little value in the Church's doctrinal formulations being true to the Biblical witness if the Biblical witness itself is not reliable. If we are to maintain that the Biblical witness is reliable, it is important to take the New Testament documents as both historically trustworthy and theologically normative.

If the New Testament is not at least substantially reliable as an historical document, then we are reduced to speculation concerning the actual nature of even the most central events of the Christian faith. For an example, consider Hick's comments on the resurrection of Jesus.

> That there was some kind of experience of seeing Jesus after his death, an appearance or appearances which came to be known as his resurrection seems virtually certain . . . But we cannot ascertain today in what this resurrection-event consisted. The possibilities range from the resuscitation of Jesus' corpse to visions of the Lord in resplendent glory.[20]

These lines are Hick's response to the claim that Jesus' resurrection sets Him apart from other men and shows Him to be God incarnate. Hick argues that this claim is difficult to sustain because the nature of the Resurrection is so uncertain. Having rejected the straightforward Biblical claim that Jesus was actually raised from the dead, Hick is at a loss to tell us what really happened. He can only surmise.

Hick believes the disciples experienced *something* after Jesus' death; but he thinks they misconstrued their experience. Now it is certainly true that those who have had vivid experiences, including religious experiences, sometimes misinterpret them.[21] Serious problems ensue, however, if we assume the apostles misconstrued such events as the Resurrection. For if we believe the Resurrection was one of the truly pivotal acts through which God revealed Himself, our claim that this is so is severely undermined if the original witnesses misconstrued it so badly that we can only guess as to its actual nature. If we want to maintain the claim that God revealed Himself in the Resurrection, it is much more plausible to assume the nature of the Resurrection was correctly perceived and described by those who witnessed and reported it.

This is suggested, moreover, by the very idea of revelation. For revelation is achieved only if the recipients of the revelation come to know what the giver of revelation wanted to make known.

Perhaps we can see this more clearly by considering that revelation, as a matter of logic, is achieved through

more basic actions. For instance, I reveal myself by
speaking, writing, gesturing, and so on. Such actions
alone, however, do not constitute revelation. Rather,
revelation is something that happens above or beyond
the basic actions or events through which it is given. For
instance, suppose I speak to you to reveal something to
you. My speaking does not constitute revelation unless
you come to know or understand what I intended to
convey by my speaking. If you misunderstand my
meaning, I did not successfully reveal myself to you.[22]

Now then, let us recall that as a result of their
experience of seeing Jesus after His death, the apostles
came to believe that He had actually been raised from the
dead. If this is not what really happened, we must
wonder whether the Resurrection was a successful act of
revelation.

This point is strengthened when we consider some of
the other beliefs the apostles held with respect to the
Resurrection. For example, they believed that Jesus had
been raised by the power of God; that His death and
resurrection made possible the salvation of all people;
that His resurrection was a pledge that believers will be
resurrected and receive a body like His glorious body.
These beliefs are closely tied to the apostolic understanding of the nature of the Resurrection.

These beliefs, however, clearly go beyond the historical question of what the disciples' experience of seeing
Jesus actually consisted of. These beliefs are theological
in nature. They involve interpretation of Jesus' death
and resurrection. How did the apostles arrive at these
beliefs?

As I have already indicated, if we are to maintain that
the Biblical witness is reliable, we must hold that the
apostolic account of Christ is theologically normative as
well as historically trustworthy. That is, we must accept as
authoritative the apostolic interpretation of the meaning
and significance of Jesus' life, death, and resurrection.

Why has the Church traditionally taken the apostolic

interpretation of the Gospel as authoritative rather than as a distortion? The answer is suggested in a number of Scripture passages. In the first place, recall that in Luke's gospel Jesus speaks with His disciples, after He has been raised, to explain to them the meaning of His death and resurrection (Luke 24:25-49). Second, the gospel of John records the promise of Jesus to His apostles that the Holy Spirit would speak to them and guide them into truth (John 14:26; 15:26; 16:12-14). Third, Paul claimed that his gospel was not something man made up, but was received by a direct revelation from Christ (Galatians 1:11-12). In short, then, the apostolic interpretation was accepted as authoritative because the Church believed that God had spoken to them and had made known to them the meaning of His action in Christ. They were not simply left to draw their own conclusions.

The whole idea of divine speaking has not been fashionable in most contemporary theology. The emphasis instead has been on revelation in history to the neglect of verbal communication. But as James Barr insisted over two decades ago, divine speaking is "an inescapable fact of the Bible . . . Direct communication from God to man has fully as much claim to be called the core of the tradition as has revelation through events in history."[23]

More recently, William J. Abraham has defended divine speaking as a crucial element in any well-rounded account of revelation. Not only is divine speaking central in Scripture, but there are good philosophical reasons also for holding to it. As Abraham points out, the concept of revelation is located primarily in the realm of interpersonal relationships. People reveal themselves to one another, and it is this which provides a model for our understanding of divine revelation. For God has been understood in the Christian tradition as a transcendent person, analogous to human persons.

In the realm of human interpersonal relationship, it is obvious that speaking plays a key role. We inform other persons of our intentions, purposes, desires, and so on by speaking. When our actions are questioned, we typically explain ourselves by speaking. Without speaking we would often be at a loss to know what others are thinking or doing. In such cases we could try to read people's intentions by observing their bodily movements. But often we would be mistaken, for bodily movements can be interpreted in several ways.[24] Of course, speaking can also be interpreted in more than one way. But it is still generally true that speaking is a more explicit mode of communication than bodily action, and is accordingly more clear.

Since God does not have a body and thus does not perform bodily movements, we are even more dependent on His speaking, if we are to know His purposes and intentions, than we are in the case of human beings. It is important to keep in mind, moreover, that divine speaking involves much more than cognitive information. God also speaks words of judgment, forgiveness, encouragement, promise, and so on. Such speaking is vital to the existential dimension of our relationship to God.

Without divine speaking, on the other hand, there seems to be little reason for thinking we can have substantial knowledge about God or our relationship to Him. Abraham expresses this point as follows.

Those who claim to know what God is doing in creation, in history, or in a world to come, and yet do this without at some point relying on their own or someone else's claim to have had direct access to the mind of God as He has revealed it, are in the dark. Incorporeal agents who do not speak are like invisible men who are dumb. We rightly are very suspicious of those who try to tell us what they are doing. We should be equally suspicious when told that such agents forgive us our sins, command us to love our neighbor, or promise us eternal life in a world to come. To express the matter thus is to say

that theologians who make claims about God's
intentions or purposes without having within their
theistic commitments a concept of direct divine
speaking are without warrants for such claims.[25]

Even if we assume, as I have argued we should, that
those who witnessed and recorded God's special acts of
revelation have given us an accurate account of those
events, this is not enough for us to know the purpose of
those acts of revelation. We still need to know *why* God
delivered the Israelites, raised Jesus from the dead, and
so on. It is because there are many ways of interpreting
the significance of such events that divine speaking is
necessary.

But again, if we are to say revelation was successfully
achieved through divine speaking, it is necessary to
assume that the apostles understood what God was
saying. As Abraham puts it, "Divine speaking and human
sensitivity together bring about divine revelation."[26] The
need for human sensitivity indicates that reason plays an
important role at the foundations of our knowledge of
God, just as experience does. For divine speaking, like
other speaking, is an activity in which one intelligence
addresses another. It is because man is an intelligent
being, endowed with reason, that he can correctly
perceive divine speaking.

Thus, if we have good reason to believe God's
revelation to the apostles included speaking, as the
Christian tradition claims, we have good reason to
believe they did not misunderstand or misconstrue
their experience of Jesus. We have good reason to
believe their theological interpretation of the Resurrection is correct. In short, we are warranted in
accepting the apostolic account of God's revelation in
Christ as theologically normative as well as historically
reliable.

The Crucial Role of Tradition and Reason

Let us turn now to a question I raised earlier in this chapter: Why must we accept the ecumenical creeds as true interpretations of Scripture if we are to maintain a substantial view of Biblical authority? For the sake of simplicity, let us limit our discussion to the Nicene creed, the most ecumenical of the ancient creeds. In that case our question can be put more sharply: Why should we accept the Nicene formulation as normative for our understanding of who Christ is? As I have already indicated, this question focuses the manner in which the authority of Scripture is interdependent with tradition and reason.

To see why this is so, let us reflect for a moment on the following premise: If Scripture is to function as an effective authority in the Church, its central meaning must be determinable and intelligible. For if the central meaning of Scripture is not both determinable and intelligible, it would be meaningless to speak of the authority of Scripture; we cannot submit to Scripture if we cannot establish its central meaning, and we cannot establish its central meaning if we cannot understand it.[27]

What this points up, clearly enough, is the crucial role which reason must play in the actual functioning of Biblical authority. Just as reason played an important role in the initial perception of revelation by prophets and apostles, so now reason must play a similar role if we are to understand the revelation they have passed on to us in the Scriptures. John Wesley emphasized this function of reason.

> The foundation of true religion stands upon the oracles of God. It is built upon the Prophets and Apostles, Jesus Christ himself being the chief corner-stone. Now, of what excellent use is reason, if we would either understand ourselves, or explain to others, those living oracles. And how is it possible

without it to understand the essential truths con-
tained therein? A beautiful summary of which we
have in what is called the Apostles' Creed. Is it not
reason (assisted by the Holy Ghost) which enables us
to understand the being and attributes of God? . . .
It is by reason that God enables us in some measure
to comprehend his method of dealing with the
children of men.[28]

It is clear from this passage that Scripture is the
ultimate religious authority for Wesley. But it is equally
plain that, for Wesley, reason plays a vital role in the
appropriation of Scripture.

Two other points are also worth noting. First, it is not
unaided reason which is the proper interpreter of
Scripture, but rather reason as assisted by the Holy
Spirit. And second, notice that Wesley draws an implicit
connection between Scripture, reason, and tradition
when he mentions the Apostles' Creed. For reason helps
us understand the essential truths of Scripture, and those
essential truths, says Wesley, are summarized in the
Apostles' Creed.

Since Scripture is understood through reason, it will
always be the case, as Wesley put it, that faith is consistent
with reason.[29] This does not mean, of course, that
everything in Scripture can be fully comprehended by
human reason. For such central doctrines as the
Incarnation and the Trinity, though we are required to
believe them since they are revealed in Scripture, are
beyond our full comprehension.[30] Nor does it mean
Scripture must be interpreted in ways which conform to
reason defined as what "modern man" finds acceptable.
As Basil Mitchell points out, this has been a mistake of
many liberal theologians. "Identifying 'reason' with some
secular system of thought, they have tended to accept
only so much of traditional Christian theism as they
believe to be consistent with 'reason' so understood; the
rest being rejected or reinterpreted."[31]

What it does mean for faith and reason to be consistent is that Scripture must be understood in such a way that inconsistency and incoherence are avoided. The message of Scripture is not only internally consistent but is also consistent with what we know outside of Scripture.

Let us turn our attention back to the Nicene Creed, and I think it will become apparent how the authority of tradition ties in with the authority of Scripture and reason. The Nicene Creed, let us recall, is the result of an intensive effort on the part of the early Church to get clear on a question which is obviously central to the Biblical revelation. It cannot be emphasized too strongly that the essential purpose of the Nicene Fathers was to state explicitly the meaning of Scripture in response to the distortion of Scriptural teaching which Arius had introduced.

Now then, if we believe Scripture is revelation from God to the Church; if we assume that the central meaning of Scripture is determinable and accessible to human reason (aided by the Holy Spirit); and if we judge the Nicene Fathers to have been capable scholars who sincerely sought to understand and maintain what Scripture teaches about Christ, then it seems to follow that their conclusions about the nature of Christ are in all likelihood a true interpretation of Scripture.

This argument is sharpened when we consider that there has been consensus on the doctrines of the Nicene Creed throughout the Church in all ages. Again and again the doctrines it proclaims have been reaffirmed as vital to the faith by theologians, by official confessions of faith adopted in various traditions, and by countless ordinary believers.

If the Nicene Creed does not faithfully express the doctrinal substance of what God intended to reveal in the Scriptures, then we must wonder why the Church throughout history has so persistently insisted upon the doctrines of the creed. Does this not raise again the question of whether Scripture can be claimed as revelation from God? For if the essential message of Scripture has been persistently misconstrued by those who have diligently sought to understand it, then Scripture fails as revelation.

The way to avoid this unhappy conclusion, as should be clear by now, is to recognize how the authorities of Scripture, tradition, and reason are interrelated. Indeed, if the Nicene Creed is a true expression of the doctrinal substance of Scripture, there is a sense in which the authority of Scripture merges with the authority of tradition. For if the creed is true to Scripture, the two are saying the same thing, so that to challenge the authority of the creed is to challenge the authority of Scripture.

To be sure, the Nicene Creed does represent a doctrinal advance, for it states the identity of Christ in an explicitly ontological mode which is only implicit in Scripture. In the words of John Courtney Murray, the creed represents "growth in understanding of the primitive affirmations in the New Testament revelation." Murray goes on to comment that:

> By thus sanctioning the principle of doctrinal growth, Nicaea established a bridge between Scripture and conciliar dogma, joining these distinct territories into the one country that is the Catholic unity of faith. Scripture states the faith of the Church; so does dogma, but in another mode of conception and statement so organically related to the Scriptural didache as to merit the name of growth.[32]

This argument can be sustained, let it be noted, without any sort of appeal to the special authority of the Church. For it is based simply on the notion that Scripture is an intelligible revelation from God.

So it is still the case that the authority of the Nicene Creed is derived from the authority of Scripture and, in this sense, is subordinate to Scripture. In principle, if it could be conclusively shown that the creed does not truly express what Scripture teaches about Christ, then the creed should be rejected. In reality, however, I do not think this is possible.

Of course, there are cases where beliefs and practices which have become common within the Church are not in accord with Scripture and should be rejected. This was the whole thrust of the Reformation. There are also cases of tradition which have only ambiguous support in Scripture. In these instances it will be legitimate to reevaluate the tradition in light of Scripture, reason, and experience. Even then it may not be altogether clear whether the tradition should be maintained or not. It is clear, however, that the authority of tradition varies from case to case. And if the Church is to remain faithful to God's revelation in Scripture, it will be necessary to keep its traditions under the searchlight of Scripture and remain open to the need for reform and correction.

Concluding Reflections

Before concluding this chapter, let us come back to the question of whether the Wesleyan Quadrilateral is a good model of authority for a Church with a policy of open-ended pluralism. The answer to this question will depend on how the four elements are ranked in relation to one another. If Scripture is taken as the primary authority and the other three criteria play a subordinate role of interpreting and confirming Scripture, then the quadrilateral will not permit open-ended pluralism. To the contrary, there will be some distinct limits on pluralism.

On the other hand, if there is no clear ranking of authority within the quadrilateral, pluralism is without bounds. As Leroy T. Howe put it:

> . . . though not indifferentist by intent, in practice the quadrilateral seems to be infinitely permis-

sive. . . . By arbitrarily defining the degree of force one or another guideline is to have in a particular discussion, one could establish almost any belief as Christian.[33]

Although United Methodism's Doctrinal Statement affirms the "primacy" of Scripture, as we have noted, the nature of this primacy is sufficiently ambiguous to allow such permissive interpretation of the quadrilateral.

However, the most significant indication of the real status of Biblical authority in our Doctrinal Statement is the fact that the central doctrines of the Christian faith are not clearly affirmed. Instead of stating clearly that Christ is God the Son incarnate, our Statement makes vague reference to "God's self-presentation in Jesus of Nazareth." In referring to the "common heritage" which United Methodists share with all other Christians of all ages, no mention is made of such prominent creedal items as the miraculous conception, bodily resurrection, and ascension of Jesus. Rather, the Statement claims only that we "honor the intent and import of the historic creeds" (p. 74).

A bit later we are reminded that "Scripture focuses on the witness to Jesus' life and teachings, his death and resurrection" (p.74). At first sight, this might appear to be an affirmation of Jesus' resurrection. However, there is a significant difference between affirming that Scripture gives witness to the Resurrection, and affirming the Resurrection itself. Even those who do not believe Christ was actually raised from the dead can heartily agree that the apostles gave witness to something which they described as resurrection.

This tentative attitude toward the central events of the New Testament revelation indicates a lack of confidence in the reality of that revelation. The lukewarm affirmation of the historic creeds is at bottom a subtle denial of Biblical authority. If we are to recover a viable sense of Biblical authority, we must regain confidence that the events recorded in Scripture really occurred, particularly the Incarnation and the events related to it. And this will entail a corresponding confidence in the historic creeds.

One predictable reaction to my proposal is that it relies too heavily on a view of divine intervention in the natural order which is no longer tenable. Ever since the Enlightenment, we may be told, appeals to traditional views of revelation have involved insurmountable problems.

While such claims as these are still made often enough, they have much less force than they used to have. This is largely due to the fact that Christian philosophers have been busily engaged for the past several years in answering many of the objections against traditional Christianity which have been common since the Enlightenment. Indeed, some of the best contemporary philosophy is written from the standpoint of traditional Christian theism.[34]

Nor is it the case that contemporary science need be an obstacle for traditional Christian belief. To the contrary, it can be argued that current scientific thinking is not only compatible with Christian orthodoxy, but can even be used to support it.[35] Thus, the view I am advocating cannot be dismissed merely by appealing to the Enlightenment.

In saying this, I am not suggesting that the problems raised by the Enlightenment should simply be ignored. Nor am I saying that nothing positive can be learned from the Enlightenment. One important gain stemming from that period is that Bible scholars have come to appreciate much more fully the complex human role in the total production of Scripture.

The point remains, however, that the Enlightenment case against special revelation, against miracles, and so on, has been effectively answered. This is a substantial gain for those who wish to retain or recover a high view of Biblical authority. The debate on these issues is still going on, to be sure, and will continue to go on. But if the current state of philosophy and science is any measure of what is theologically acceptable, the way is wide open for the classical Christian tradition to be reclaimed.

If United Methodists are among those who recover a strong sense of Biblical authority, there is good reason to believe the quadrilateral will be a helpful instrument for addressing the crisis of authority in contemporary theology. On the other hand, if a vital sense of Biblical authority is not recovered, there is good reason to suspect the quadrilateral will continue to be used primarily as a tool in the hands of those who wish to evade the claims of historic Christianity.

6

PLURALISM, DOCTRINAL STANDARDS, AND THE NATURE OF THEOLOGY

Theologians commonly draw a distinction between doctrine and theology. While it is important to recognize that the two are related, their differences also must be kept clearly in mind. Geoffrey Wainwright has succinctly expressed the distinction between doctrine and theology:

> Doctrine or dogma refers to official formulations of the faith which have become classical but which are conceivably not the only ways of stating the faith. Theology refers to the more individual but still ecclesial activity of reflecting on faith and doctrine with a view to their intellectual clarification.[1]

There are other ways to define these terms and other ways to draw the distinction between them. Theology, in particular, is variously defined by different theologians. But the point for emphasis here is that doctrinal formulations serve as official standards for entire

Christian communities, while theology, generally speaking, is a more individual effort to clarify and express the faith. Of course, theology is not an altogether individual effort, for it is normally done in community with other scholars and theologians.

Somewhat surprisingly, as was noted in chapter two, our *Discipline* does not seem to distinguish between theology and doctrine. The two terms, though not explicitly identified, are used interchangeably throughout the Doctrinal Statement. And while it contains a good deal about the nature and importance of theology, there seems to be no recognition of the vital but distinct role which doctrinal standards should play in the life of the church.

Ogden: A Needless Dilemma

Shortly after the 1972 Statement was adopted, Schubert M. Ogden published an essay in which he argued at length that the failure of the Statement to distinguish between the role of theology and the role of doctrinal standards created an unnecessary dilemma.[2] The dilemma stems from the perfectly legitimate desire on the part of the authors of the Statement to maintain both a measure of doctrinal discipline in the church as well as adequate freedom for theologians to carry out their task. In order to achieve this balance, the Statement attempts to chart "a course between doctrinal dogmatism on the one hand and doctrinal indifferentism on the other" (p. 82).

Unfortunately, however, our Statement does not achieve the balance it professes to achieve. In actuality, the Statement is far more concerned with the problem of dogmatism than with indifferentism. As Ogden put it, the Statement is "excessively preoccupied with avoiding doctrinal rigidity, literalness, and inflexibility" but is "rather less" worried about the opposite dangers of indifferentism. This excessive concern with dogmatism, moreover, is hardly an accurate reflection of the actual situation in our church. For in reality, doctrinal indifferentism is a much greater threat to us than dogmatism. "It is notorious that, at every level in the church, from the local congregation to the General Conference, it is possible to disseminate the widest range of doctrines, both theological and ethical, regardless of the extent of their contrariety to the doctrinal standards we have officially acknowledged."[3]

Ogden's chief criticism, however, centers on the dilemma involved in wanting to maintain both discipline and freedom. As he sees it, theological freedom and doctrinal discipline are understood in our Statement in such a way "that they can only be played off against one another." The result is that our doctrinal standards are assigned a role which is "far from the role of being standards of doctrine in the proper sense of the words."[4] This is apparent, Ogden notes, from the fact that our Statement insists that the doctrinal standards cited in the first two Restrictive Rules[5] "are not to be construed literally and juridically." Henceforth, doctrinal reflection is to be carried out by "free inquiry" within the boundaries of Scripture, tradition, reason, and experience (p. 78; cf. pp. 49; 82).

This result is clearly unacceptable for Ogden, for he thinks that it is essential for a church to have explicit standards of doctrine in order to measure the adequacy of its continuing witness. The effectiveness of a church's witness, moreover, depends on the cooperation of its individual members. For every individual who is confirmed as a member of a Christian church accepts responsibility to share in the witness of the church, and part of this responsibility involves accountability to the doctrinal standards of that church. Without such accountability, the witness of the church suffers.

Now, how does Ogden maintain such a view of doctrinal standards without playing it off against theological freedom? The answer lies in his view of the role of theology, which he sharply distinguishes from the role of official church doctrine. Ogden's view of the role of theology is rather novel, for as he recognizes, it is a departure from the understanding of theology which has been held throughout most of Church history. The traditional view, according to Ogden, is that theology serves the Church by formulating the Church's witness in conceptual terms.

Over against this traditional view, Ogden insists that if theology is to play its proper role, it must be independent of the Church. The work of theology cannot be effectively carried out unless theologians are guaranteed freedom. Thus, theology—as opposed to doctrine—is properly characterized as "free inquiry" within the boundaries of Scripture, tradition, reason, and experience. Theological development cannot, however, be properly restricted to "the framework of our doctrinal heritage" (cf. Discipline, p. 82). For if theology is bound by the United Methodist doctrinal heritage, it cannot really be free inquiry limited only by the quadrilateral. Ogden spells out his position quite explicitly, as follows.

> The point I wish to insist on is that the only theology the United Methodist Church or any other Christian church has any reason to promote is a theology which is not itself subject to the discipline of any church's doctrinal standards. Theology is not subject to such standards, namely because, properly understood, its task is precisely the critical understanding, and, as may be, correction of those very standards by reference to the basic norms of Scripture and tradition, on the one hand, and experience and reason, on the other.[6]

When the independence of theology is thus recognized, according to Ogden, it is impossible to play off theological freedom against doctrinal responsibility. Indeed, he thinks the only way to break out of the dilemma of purchasing freedom at the cost of responsibility is by recognizing the independent nature of theology.

In short then, while Ogden thinks it is vital for a church's witness for it to have definite doctrinal standards, he thinks theologians must be exempt from those standards. For it is the very nature of the theological task that it cannot be properly carried out if theologians must be accountable to official church doctrine.[7]

Cushman: Doctrine Displaced by Theology

Not long after Ogden's essay appeared, Robert E. Cushman published an incisive critique of the 1972 Doctrinal Statement.[8] He too focuses on the role which the Statement assigns to theology and its relation to doctrinal standards.

Cushman begins his critique by noting that it is both implicit and explicit throughout the Statement that the whole church is responsible to share in the tasks of theologizing and doctrinal formulation. All members of the United Methodist Church are expected "to accept the challenge of responsible theological reflection" (p. 82). The "principle of local initiative in the church's theological task" is fully spelled out and supported.

This includes encouragement for "informed theological experimentation." The *Discipline* reminds us, however, that local initiatives can only be taken seriously if they meet two conditions: "careful regard for our heritage and fourfold guidelines, and the double test of acceptability and edification in corporate worship and common life" (p. 83).

What all this amounts to, as Cushman observes, is "a species of intramural conciliarism as the source and authorization of doctrinal standards."[9] The whole church, so to speak, is on the council which authorizes doctrine.

While this picture may appeal to our democratic instincts, it raises serious questions. Are there any restrictions on all this theological experimentation? How are we to understand the condition of "careful regard for our heritage"? What is the actual status of our doctrinal heritage with respect to the theological task?

A particularly revealing passage from our Doctrinal Statement in this regard is the following, which explains how we should now view the historic doctrinal confessions of the United Methodist tradition.

> They are and ought to remain as important landmarks in our complex heritage and ought rightly to be retained in the *Discipline.* . . . But, since they are not accorded any status of finality, either in content or rhetoric, there is no objection in principle to the continued development of still other doctrinal summaries and liturgical creeds that may gain acceptance and use in the church — without displacing those we already have. This principle of the historical interpretation of all doctrinal statements, past and present, is crucial (p. 50).

What this passage makes clear is that our Statement does not regard our traditional doctrinal confessions as normative standards for contemporary believers. To the contrary, these confessions are expressly denied "any status of finality" (cf. also p. 41). We should look to them, says the *Discipline,* only as "important landmarks in our complex heritage." Indeed, later in our Doctrinal Statement the historic creeds of Christendom are also relegated—along with our traditional confessions—to the status of "cherished landmarks of Christian self-consciousness and affirmation" (p. 83).

Given this view of our historic doctrinal creeds and confessions, what can "careful regard for our heritage" amount to? Apparently it involves little more than having some awareness of the landmarks which have given guidance, along the way, to previous generations of believers.

Crucial to this understanding of the classical creeds and confessions is the "principle of the historical interpretation of all doctrinal statements." In a similar vein we are informed in another context that: "Our newer historical consciousness allows us to retain the various landmarks of our several heritages, interpreting them in historical perspective" (p. 73).

But just what is this "principle of historical interpretation"? The answer is by no means clear. As crucial as the principle is alleged to be, it is not spelled out for us. Cushman, however, seems to be on target when he says the meaning is that all historic documents, including our traditional confessions, "are relative to their given context and so without finality."[10] The consequence of this relativism is far-reaching indeed. "It is this hermeneutical principle that banishes any status of finality for [doctrinal] standards and opens the door to horizons unlimited in theological development."[11]

What, then, is the relationship between theology and doctrinal standards? As Cushman sees it, the relationship is actually one of replacement. That is, our Statement, whether intentionally or not, tends to replace all doctrine, past, present or future, with an open-ended process of theologizing.

> In this perspective, is it something like the case that the church is now to live perpetually on theological credit? In reflection one is inclined to wonder whether the authors of this document either did not fully understand their own logic as a committee, or that some did, and because they had relinquished any possibility of standards had resorted to collective "theologizing" as a permanent substitute for doctrine. Yet this seems to be the outcome of the logic employed, however awkward the new day in which the church is obliged to rely mainly for truths to live

by upon the ever-receding promise of the future.[12]

Cushman obviously views this development as an unsatisfactory way for the church to secure "truths to live by". Even if the whole church were to accept the challenge to engage in theological reflection and experimentation, this would not be an adequate replacement for official doctrine.

An Assessment

As the analyses of Ogden and Cushman made clear, a serious and unresolved tension exists in our Doctrinal Statement between theological freedom and doctrinal discipline. This tension is largely generated by confusion over the proper role of theology. For the remainder of this chapter, I want to discuss the nature of the theological task in relation to the role of doctrine, and the connected question of freedom and discipline.

To begin, I think our discussion thus far does show that doctrine should be distinguished from theology. The distinction between the two is not always clear and in some cases it would be artificial to press it. Nevertheless, it is helpful to separate them, especially when the question concerns their role in the life of the church.

One way to focus the difference between them is to say whereas doctrine may be accorded a status of finality, theology should not be conceived in such terms. The notion that doctrine can be accorded a status of finality follows from the conviction that the central meaning and message of Scripture is determinable. To say the central meaning of Scripture is determinable is to say it can be established. As we noted in the last chapter, there has been a consensus throughout the church that the central doctrinal message of Scripture was established in the early creeds. Thus, the doctrinal consensus expressed in the creeds can be accorded a status of finality.

Let us explore this point by drawing on John Courtney

Murray's analysis of how the Nicene formulation, that Christ is *homoousios* with the Father, represents a doctrinal finality. According to Murray's analysis, the Nicene formulation successfully avoided two fallacies, which he calls "archaism" and "futurism."

The archaists objected to the *homoousion* on the grounds that it is not a Biblical term. According to this objection, only express Biblical formulas may be used in stating the Christian faith. "At the root of the fallacy is the rejection of the notion that Christian understanding of the affirmations of the faith can and indeed must grow, at the same time that the sense of the affirmations remains unaltered."[13]

While the archaist view was conservative in one sense, in a more important sense it was not, for it actually failed to conserve the Scriptural teaching about Christ. As Murray points out, the problem was that the Arians were willing to recite the Scriptural affirmations about Christ, but they read into them an Arian understanding, namely, that the Son of God is a creature. Therefore, the Nicene Fathers had to spell out the sense of Scripture in a manner which was sufficiently explicit to rule out the Arian understanding.

To reject the Nicene formula was not only to refuse to rule out the Arian understanding of Jesus' sonship, but also to leave the door open to other misunderstandings as well. Thus, archaism naturally leads to futurism.

> The futurist fallacy rests on the notion that the affirmations of Christian faith never have a final sense. They are constantly subject to reinterpretation in terms of any sort of philosophical thought. Development in the understanding of them is altogether open-ended. It may move in any direction, even to the dissolution of the original sense of the Christian affirmations.[14]

In affirming that Scripture has a sense which can be

determined and which places definite limits on interpretation, the Nicene Fathers repudiated the futurist fallacy.

Our Doctrinal Statement, on the other hand, with its affirmation of the principle of historical interpretation; with its notion that the classic creeds are mere "landmarks" with no status of finality; with its reliance, as Cushman put it, "on the ever-receding promise of the future," apparently embraces with both arms the fallacy of futurism.[15]

If doctrinal standards are to have any real authority among us, we cannot accept the notion that all doctrinal statements are mere landmarks. Rather, we must insist that some doctrinal statements express truth, and are thus final.

This is not to say, however, that the particular language of those statements is final. Thus, to come back to the creed, it is not the case that the Nicene formula is the only way to express the Nicene doctrine. There may be other terminology, other philosophical concepts which can express the same doctrine. Thus, the Nicene *formula* is not final in the sense that there is no other adequate way to say who Christ is. But the *doctrine* is final, and if any other terminology is proposed it must be shown that its meaning is equivalent to the Nicene formula.[16] And indeed, it is part of the ongoing task of theology to search for other concepts and terminology which will effectively communicate the meaning of terms such as the *homoousion*.

Thus it is the case, as our Doctrinal Statement puts it, that our theological task is "never ending" (p. 78). But if we are to keep theology distinct from doctrine, we must be clear on why this is so. It is not because nothing is settled and we must therefore be on an endless quest in search of truth which forever eludes us. Rather, the truth of the Gospel has been given to us. It does not need to be discovered but has been successfully revealed. Nevertheless, the truth of the Gospel must be grasped and appropriated afresh in every generation. It is part of the theological task to make this possible.

But of course the Gospel is not addressed, strictly speaking, to generations, but rather to individuals. It is individuals who must grasp and appropriate the Gospel afresh in every generation. And this points up the sense in which we may reasonably expect all Christians "to accept the challenge of responsible theological reflection." For it is part of the essential business of Christian living to think correctly about God and to understand His will for our lives. Such understanding is vital if we are to apply the Gospel to everyday life.

Paul L. Holmer has suggested that learning theology is like learning grammar or logic. One studies grammar, for instance, not as an end in itself but to enable one to speak grammatically. The aim is not simply to learn the rules but to gain competence to speak correctly about all sorts of things. And just as we learn grammar in order to speak grammatically, so we learn theology in order to be godly. "This is how it is, then, with theology—namely, that we are to become godly in all things, referring everything, our woes and weal, fears and joys, past and future, completely to God's love and care."[17]

What should be expected of believers, then, is not that they should engage in theological experimentation with the latest fads and novelties, but that they should learn the "grammar of faith" well enough to live thoroughly godly lives. Learning the grammar of faith involves attaining a firm grasp of what Holmer calls that "singular and corelike Christianity" which is the same from age to age.[18]

In view of this, we should be dubious of our Doctrinal Statement's claim that: "No single creed or doctrinal summary can adequately serve the needs and intentions of United Methodists in confessing their faith or in celebrating their Christian experience" (p. 83). For it is that essential "corelike Christianity" which is expressed in our historic creeds and doctrinal confessions. The classic creeds and confessions lay out the basic framework of the faith, and it is no more the case that we need multiple creeds than that we need multiple sets of grammatical rules.

Many different matters can be addressed and discussed, and in a remarkable variety of styles, by those who have mastered the rules of grammar. And in a similar way, that corelike Christianity is resilient enough to be applied by individual believers in a whole host of circumstances, and its implications can be drawn out in more ways than we have yet seen. So, individual expression of Christian faith and experience comes at the level of applying the grammar of faith, not at the level of inventing a new grammar.

This suggests another reason why the theological task is an ongoing one, namely, because "theological reflections do change as Christians become aware of new issues and crises" (p. 82). While this is an important point, we must be careful to consider just what it entails. Many theologians, in their desire to keep Christianity relevant to new issues, have thought it necessary to change or adapt Christianity. Thus, theologians have often accommodated the faith to prevailing trends to the point that their proposals are hardly recognizable as Christian theology. For those who think Christianity makes ultimate truth claims, this is not an acceptable way to carry out the theological task. As Holmer remarks:

> Unlike the popular everyday view that theology must always adapt and must always be contemporary, we must insist that theology proposes something that is timeless and eternal. Instead of using popular causes and ideas of the day and then clothing them in the language of faith, the task of theology is to construe those causes and ideas, their feasibility and truth, in relation to God and his way among men. It is in this way that Christianity stays

always relevant, for nothing human is outside of God's purview and dominion.[19]

So it is one thing to say *theological reflections* change as we become aware of new issues, but it is another thing altogether to say *basic Christian doctrine* must be changed in order to be relevant to new issues. For it is no more necessary for theologians to change basic Christian doctrine in order to address new issues than it would be for a politician to change basic English grammar in order to address new issues.

This brings us back again to the point that if doctrinal standards are to have any real authority among us, some doctrinal affirmations must be recognized as expressing final truth. This means, furthermore, that some doctrinal affirmations represent a limit to theological freedom. If the tension in our Doctrinal Statement between discipline and freedom is to be resolved, it must be frankly recognized that we cannot have both serious doctrinal standards and unlimited freedom. Although our Statement tries to have it both ways, as both Cushman and Ogden pointed out, doctrine is displaced by theology, and discipline loses out to freedom.

One of the purposes of doctrinal standards is to define the boundaries of theological freedom. This has certainly been the case with doctrinal standards in our heritage, going back originally to Wesley's Model Deed which placed some doctrinal restrictions on those who used his chapels. As our Doctrinal Statement explains: "The aim here [with the Model Deed] was not to impose an inflexible system of doctrine or to inhibit responsible intellectual freedom, but rather to provide a broad and flexible framework of doctrine which would define the outside limits for public teaching in the societies in disputed cases" (p. 42). The point I want to insist on is that it is inevitable that there will be cases of conflict between theological freedom and doctrinal standards, and if those standards are taken seriously it is freedom which must give way in such cases.

Yet, if this is so, doesn't it imperil the whole theological task? As we recall, Ogden argued that the conflict between theological freedom and doctrinal discipline disappears if we recognize that the nature of theology is such that theologians should not be accountable to official doctrinal standards. For it is part of the theological task to critique and even correct those standards. This means that United Methodist theology must be free inquiry, bound only by the fourfold criteria of the quadrilateral.

While Ogden's proposal seems to provide an easy way out of a difficult dilemma, I do not think it is a satisfactory solution to the problems it addresses. In the first place, I do not think his move to make theology independent from the Church is acceptable. This move, to be sure, is right in line with the whole tendency of many contemporary theologians to view themselves primarily as members of the academy and only secondarily as churchmen. As a result, much modern theology is far removed from the actual life and work of the Church.

Since I view this as an unfortunate development, I am inclined to agree with Wainwright's definition, cited above, which conceives of theology as a "more individual but still ecclesial activity." In the following, Wainwright points out one of the ways in which theology should contribute to the mission of the Church.

> Those who put questions on behalf of the "simple believer" often ask the professional theologian, with doubt in their voice, whether his theology "can be preached." The question is mistaken if it implies that there ought properly to be a simple equation between theology and preaching. But it is justified in so far as it requires that theology should serve the Church's proclamation.[20]

In the second place, Ogden's proposal does not come

to grips with the fact that the quadrilateral places significant limitations on theological freedom, at least if Scripture is recognized as primary. Indeed, as I argued in the preceding chapter, the quadrilateral strongly supports the central doctrines of traditional Christianity. Thus, it will not do to drive a wedge, as Ogden wants to do, between theology as free inquiry within the bounds of the quadrilateral and theology which is accountable to our official doctrinal standards. For the quadrilateral represents essentially the same boundary as our doctrinal standards.

The most serious problem with Ogden's proposal, however, is that it is still in serious tension with the doctrinal discipline which Ogden himself believes is necessary to a church's witness. For if theologians are granted exemption from doctrinal discipline, it is simply unrealistic to think that such discipline can be maintained in the rest of the church.

Ogden rightly decries the fact that doctrine which is flatly contrary to our acknowledged standards can be promulgated at every level of the church. What he doesn't seem to recognize, however, is that this is largely a reflection of the fact that theologians all across our church are teaching doctrine, and advocating theological positions, which contradict even the most basic tenets of the Christian faith.[21] For theologians teach pastors, and pastors teach laymen. What this suggests is not that theologians should have a special status of exemption from accountability to doctrinal standards, but rather that it is especially important that they be held accountable.

In saying this, I do not mean to suggest that there is no merit whatsoever to Ogden's view that part of the task of theology is to criticize and even correct official doctrine. For it may well be that some articles in our historic United Methodist doctrinal confessions should be revised or amended. Not all articles in those confessions have the same status of finality. Some articles clearly affirm essential Christian doctrine, while others deal with more peripheral matters. I would suggest that theologians should be free to "think and let think," as Wesley put it, on matters "which do not strike at the roots of Christianity." But even granting this, there are some clear lines which cannot be crossed.

Nor do I mean to suggest that theologians or seminary professors should be coerced to believe something they do not really believe. To the contrary, I would argue that it is the right of all men, including theologians, to think for themselves and embrace whatever conclusions they believe true. In the process of such thinking, theologians may come to reject beliefs they formerly accepted. Free inquiry in this sense, I would urge, is not bound even by the quadrilateral. For a theologian may honestly come to believe things which are not warranted by the quadrilateral. Indeed, he may come to the conclusion that Christianity is false, or even that God does not exist. On the other hand, he may become even more convinced that traditional Christianity is true. It is part of the risk of honest inquiry that one cannot be sure where his thinking will lead him.

But it does not follow from this that anyone has the right to a teaching office in the church if he believes things that are contrary to the basic doctrines of the church. That is the real issue here. For the church has the right, nay, the responsibility to maintain doctrinal discipline. To suggest that such discipline is an undue infringement of academic freedom is to indicate that one is committed to a notion of intellectual autonomy which is shaped more by secular ideals than by Christian truth.

Before turning to consider the difficult practical questions which arise from our discussion in this section, let us take a moment to summarize our conclusions. The central thrust of this section is that it is vital to get clear on the nature and task of theology in order to address the issue of theological pluralism. Fundamental to the argument was the distinction between doctrine and theology. In view of this distinction, we may affirm theological pluralism while repudiating doctrinal pluralism, for basic doctrine defines the limits of theological pluralism.

Legitimate theological pluralism is primarily the product of the need to communicate the Gospel afresh in every generation and to apply the Gospel to new circumstances and issues which arise. While it is important for theologians to have significant freedom to explore ideas and different ways of interpreting the faith, theologians too must be accountable to essential Christian doctrine. This is based on the understanding of theology as an ecclesial activity which should serve the Church in its mission to the world.

The Church should not, however, jump to hasty conclusions when evaluating innovative theological programs. For individual theologians have often pioneered the way with important insights which were overlooked or ignored by the rest of the Church. It is not always clear, at least initially, whether new ideas proposed by such pioneers are legitimate expressions or developments of the faith, on the one hand, or aberrations on the other. In such cases, debate should continue until consensus may be reached. This should not obscure the fact, however, that some theological proposals are clearly incompatible with essential Christian doctrine. Such proposals should be firmly rejected.[22]

The Thorny Practical Question

What should be done when a theologian, pastor, official board member, or bishop holds and teaches views which are incompatible with basic church doctrine? If we have no response to this question, the preceding discussion is largely pointless.

While there are no simple answers, perhaps the solution with most integrity is for the person involved frankly to admit where he stands and to resign his office.

This would be the intellectually honest thing to do, and the church should accept such resignations with both respect and regret. Indeed, the church should exercise sensitivity in such cases and do what it can to help such persons make the transition to some other vocation.

Resignations from church office because of disagreements with doctrine are relatively rare, however. Those whose views are at odds with official doctrine usually choose to remain in office and, indeed, often insist upon the right to do so. Does the church have any effective recourse for dealing with such persons?

Legally speaking, the answer is surely yes. Our *Discipline* contains provisions for taking official action against persons who disseminate "doctrines contrary to the established doctrines of the United Methodist Church" (p. 616). But the very suggestion that such action might be appropriate in these times makes most United Methodists quite uneasy. For the idea dredges up images of the Inquisition, or of "witch hunts" in which narrow-minded churchmen lower the boom on creative and courageous thinkers who desire merely to follow the truth wherever it leads. In such an atmosphere an official trial over doctrine would likely be counterproductive.

As an alternative to such official action, Thomas Oden has suggested that pastoral admonition is a workable tool in the realm of doctrinal discipline.

> Is it too much to ask or hope that some judicatories or bishops or credentials committees or boards of ministry will have the courage on occasion to inquire about alleged flagrant abuses of the teaching office? Or, on serious and fair examination, if the fulmination against Christian doctrine should continue, would it not then be reasonable for a judicatory to ask the teacher to show cause why the credential should be continued, or how the person might properly be supervised or pastorally advised in the interest of the Christian community?[23]

It is worth remembering that every bishop consecrated in the United Methodist Church takes a vow affirming that he is ready "to defend the Church against all doctrine contrary to God's Word."[24] In view of this vow, it does not seem unreasonable to expect that our bishops would engage in the kind of pastoral admonition proposed by Oden. Indeed, if they would do so with a spirit of love and a genuine concern for the persons they lead, it seems likely that the whole church would ultimately benefit.

We focus too readily on the fact that the exercise of discipline is sometimes painful, disruptive, and even divisive. It should be recognized, however, that serious problems are also occasioned by the *failure* to exercise discipline. In our desire to avoid the unpleasant aspects of discipline, we too easily forget this fact.

Consider the point made by Anglican Tom Wright that the question of doctrinal standards has to do not merely with the right to a teaching office of those persons who cannot assent to the Church's doctrine, but also with the "tender consciences" of those who believe that truth matters and that the Church has a responsibility to stand for truth.

> One can envisage the possibility that, in the not too distant future, a bishop may be faced with a choice: either to withdraw his license from someone whose deliberate and considered teaching cuts directly against the Church's formularies in general as well as in detail, or to fail to do so, and thus actually to "unchurch" those who find it in conscience . . . intolerable to stay in a place where such teaching flourishes unchecked. Indeed, one fears that the latter alternative, though less dramatic, shocking, or headline catching than the former, may have been happening already. . . . Comments like this will, of course, raise hackles. But the underlying issues will not go away, and the problem of two dogmatisms, the one in favor of declared doctrine, the other

opposed to it, may well be our modern version of problems faced by our forefathers ever since the Reformation. At its heart, this is a question about the nature of the Church.[25]

This should certainly cause us to think twice, especially in light of the fact that our United Methodist Church has lost tens of thousands of members annually for the past several years.

It is commonly assumed that if doctrinal discipline were applied, it would cause controversy all across our church and many persons would leave as a result. Fear of this possibility no doubt accounts partly for the reluctance to exercise discipline. And this fear is not altogether unfounded. Surely some persons would leave out of protest if we began to take doctrinal discipline seriously.

The question we must ask, however, is why there is no concern for those persons who are leaving our ranks precisely because we do *not* exercise discipline. Of course, not all persons who leave do so because of our doctrinal and moral laxity, but it is hard to deny that this is a significant factor, particularly in view of the fact that more conservative churches have grown steadily during our period of decline.[26]

The question can be put even more bluntly: Why is our church more concerned to maintain the membership of those who want the freedom to deny basic Christian doctrine than the membership of those who believe such doctrine should be conscientiously maintained?

We are back, then, to the "two dogmatisms." We are confronted again with the conflict between theological freedom and doctrinal discipline. We must face the dilemma of choosing either unlimited theological freedom or doctrinal discipline. We must select one horn of the dilemma or the other, and which horn we take will reveal our understanding of the nature of the Church.

Is it or is it not essential to the Church that it have explicit doctrinal standards, not only to proclaim its faith to the world, but also to discipline its continuing witness to that faith? This is the bottom line, and questions of membership gain or loss are incidental in comparison.

EPILOGUE

I began this book by reflecting on the fact that United Methodism's bicentennial celebration was clouded somewhat by a mood of uncertain direction and identity. To its credit, the 1984 General Conference took steps to try to restore the sense of direction and identity we have lost by appointing commissions to study afresh our Doctrinal Statement and the nature of our mission. The hope is that these studies will lead to a consensus which will enable us to be truly united as we face the tasks which lie before us.

This book was written out of the conviction that doctrinal unity is essential to any meaningful consensus we may hope to achieve. It is crucial that we reclaim our doctrinal heritage if we are ever to experience genuine renewal.

I want to emphasize, however, that genuine renewal involves much more than doctrinal recovery. While sound doctrine is certainly one dimension of renewal, it is only one. There are other matters, not doctrinal in nature, which must be addressed if our church is to regain its vitality. One of the most important of these is our need to be open to the work of the Holy Spirit. This was recently stressed by Bishop Ole E. Borgen.

A renewed emphasis on a deepened spiritual life, where the gifts of the Holy Spirit are functioning and the fruits of the Spirit are made visible, is essential for the strengthening and growth of the church. Renewal is basically a spiritual matter.[1]

In light of this reality, no one should view the prospect of a new Doctrinal Statement as a magic cure for our current lethargy.

Indeed, it would be unrealistic to think that even our doctrinal problems would be solved merely by the adoption of a new Doctrinal Statement. Albert C. Outler's reminder to the 1972 General Conference remains true today: "Doctrinal confusion cannot be overcome by official dogmatic pronouncement."[2] Our doctrinal confusion was not created overnight and it will not be eliminated overnight. We should be under no illusion that we can repair all our doctrinal difficulties quickly and easily.

None of this, however, should distract us from the fact that we must restore our doctrinal moorings. For what a church confesses to believe is integral to all phases of its life. To illustrate this point, let us recall a passage from our Doctrinal Statement which I have already quoted.

> . . . there is . . . general agreement that the United Methodist Church stands urgently in need of doctrinal reinvigoration for the sake of authentic renewal, fruitful evangelism, and the effective discharge of our ecumenical commitments. Seen in this light, the recovery and updating of our distinctive doctrinal heritage—"truly catholic, truly evangelical, and truly reformed"—takes on a high priority (p. 50).

Let us briefly consider how doctrine is integral to such central activities in the life of the church as evangelism and ecumenism.

Our need to engage in fruitful evangelism is even more apparent now than it was over a dozen years ago when the passage above was written. This is largely due to the fact that our church has experienced steady decline over this period. It is increasingly recognized that evangelism is vital not only for the health of our church but even for its very existence. Consequently, a new emphasis on evangelism has arisen throughout United Methodism.

It remains to be seen however, what this new emphasis really amounts to. Are we witnessing a genuinely revitalized commitment to carry out our Lord's mandate to preach the Gospel to all people? Or is our evangelism merely being used as a means of institutional survival?

One thing seems clear to me: Our doctrinal ambiguity creates a sense of ambivalence about the new thrust toward evangelism in our church. It is hard to take seriously the call to evangelism when we are so uncertain and inconsistent in maintaining the doctrines which are the heart and soul of the evangelistic enterprise. The call to evangelism will inevitably ring hollow so long as this is the case. Indeed, the extensive disagreement over what evangelism even means is largely due, I suspect, to our doctrinal equivocation.

The heart of the Good News is that God loved us enough to become incarnate in the person of His Son and die for our sins. Another crucial aspect of the Gospel is the Christian hope of eternal life, which hinges on the belief that Christ was raised bodily from the dead. Because He was, so shall we be. And the message that even now our lives can be transformed is warranted by the belief that Christ ascended to the right hand of the Father and poured out the Holy Spirit on the Church.

Evangelism is muffled to the extent that doctrines such as these are denied, or only vaguely or unreliably taught and proclaimed. Effective evangelism cannot proceed without hearty commitment to the essential doctrines of historic Christianity.

It is quite obvious that doctrine is also a matter of vital importance in ecumenical endeavors. It is because doctrine is taken seriously that ecumenism is often so elusive. Differences between Christian traditions at the doctrinal level are not easily resolved.

However, it is important to keep in mind that ecumenical aspirations are grounded in the substantial doctrinal unity which all Christian traditions already share. Because we agree on several matters of great importance, there is reason to hope that remaining differences are not insuperable.

But if the doctrines which unite Christians of different traditions are not conscientiously maintained, the ground of ecumenism is undercut. Anglican theologian J.I. Packer made this point recently with reference to Protestant-Catholic relations.

> . . .until the cancerous spread of theological plural-
> ism on both sides of the Reformation divide is
> stopped, any talk of our having achieved unity of
> faith will be so irrelevant to the real situation as to be
> both comic and pathetic. Comic because it will be so
> false, and pathetic because the unity formulas will at
> once be swallowed and relativized by the socio-secu-
> larist juggernaut ideology which is currently de-
> vouring the true, intended sense of formulas of faith
> in our separate circles of communion.[3]

So it is just as necessary for true ecumenism that we remain firm on basic doctrine as it is that we be tolerant and flexible on secondary issues.

Other examples besides evangelism and ecumenism could be cited to illustrate the point, but I think it is reasonably clear what I mean when I say doctrine is integral to all phases of the life of the church. Doctrine is not a mere theoretical concern which has nothing to do with practical concerns facing the church.

It is very fitting, in this light, that our church is re-examining the nature of its mission at the same time that it is re-examining its Doctrinal Statement. For these matters surely go together. Insofar as we are indefinite in our beliefs, we are likely to be uncertain about the nature of our mission. And if we hope to regain a clear sense of our mission as a church, we must regain a corresponding doctrinal clarity. We cannot recover our purpose and direction if we do not also recover our identity.

I want to propose that we could take a major step in this direction by forthrightly reaffirming the doctrines of the ecumenical creeds, namely, the Apostles' and Nicene. This step is crucial for the "recovery and updating of our distinctive doctrinal heritage—'truly catholic, truly evangelical, and truly reformed.' "

Our Statement has provided us with a helpful summary of the evangelical-reformed side of our doctrinal heritage. This is particularly so in the section headed "Distinctive Emphases of United Methodists," where we have a concise account of Wesley's evangelical account of salvation (pp. 75-78).

However, our Statement is not so faithful to the catholic side of our doctrinal heritage. This weakness is apparent in the section on "United Methodists and the Christian Tradition." We are reminded in this section that "We share a common heritage with all other Christians everywhere and in all ages" (p. 73). Unfortunately, in what follows, the doctrines of this common heritage are not clearly affirmed. It is the historic creeds above all which epitomize the common Christian heritage, and our Statement claims with respect to the creeds, only that we honor their "intent and import" (p. 74).

This is not sufficient to make good our profession to be catholic in doctrine. Truly to demonstrate doctrinal catholicity, we must adhere steadily to the doctrines of the creeds. If we are not prepared to stand fast on these doctrines, we cannot maintain our claim to share in the common faith of all Christians in all ages.

In calling for a forthright reaffirmation of the creeds, I do not mean to suggest that we should ignore or downplay our evangelical distinctives. Quite the contrary. Indeed, I would urge that the truth of our evangelical distinctives is most evident when they are seen in relation to the foundational catholic doctrines which underlie them. An obvious example of this point is the theology of John Wesley. For he developed his own powerful version of evangelical theology as Rupert E. Davies put it, "within the firm framework of the creeds."[4]

If we can learn from Wesley at this juncture, and successfully recover our full doctrinal heritage—catholic as well as evangelical and reformed; and if we can acquire a clear understanding of our mission, firmly grounded in our doctrinal identity; then we may achieve the sort of consensus which will enable our church to move forward with purpose and conviction.

NOTES

Introduction

1. Leonard I. Sweet, "The Four Fundamentalisms of Oldline Protestantism," *The Christian Century*, March 13, 1985, p. 266. United Seminary is a United Methodist school in Dayton, Ohio.
2. *United Methodist Reporter (UMR)*, May 4, 1984, p. 3.
3. *UMR*, May 18, 1984, p. 3.
4. James V. Heidinger highlights a number of important aspects of the problem in his editorial, "The Problem of Pluralism," *Good News*, May/June 1982, pp. 35-39. See also Heidinger's "What Do We United Methodists Believe?" *Good News*, January/February 1985, pp. 6-7.
5. Emerson Colaw, *Beliefs of a United Methodist Christian*, Tidings, Nashville, 1972, pp. 11, 13, 14.
6. The Restrictive Rules in question read as follows:
   Article I. — The General Conference shall not revoke, alter, or change our Articles of Religion or establish any new standards or rules of doctrine contrary to our present existing and established standards of doctrine.
   Article II. — The General Conference shall not revoke, alter, or change our Confession of Faith. (*Discipline*, 1984, p. 25)
7. *Beliefs of a United Methodist Christian*, p. 12.
8. The doctrinal standards referred to, apparently, are Wesley's *Standard Sermons* and *Notes Upon the New Testament*, along with The Articles of Religion of the Methodist Church and the Confession of Faith of the Evangelical United Brethren Church. There is not much force in appealing to these standards for mere "guidance."
9. *Good News*, March/April 1981, p. 64.
10. "The Problem of Pluralism," p. 35.
11. *Drifted Astray*, Abingdon, Nashville, 1983, p. 55.
12. "What We Believe," *The Interpreter*, March/April 1982, p. 8.
13. A detailed account of how American Methodist theology evolved from the time of Wesley into the early twentieth century is provided by Robert E. Chiles in *Theological Transition in American Methodism: 1790-1935*, Lanham, Maryland, University Press of America, 1983. (Originally published by Abingdon Press in 1965.)
14. James Hastings Nichols, *History of Christianity: 1650-1950*, The Ronald Press, New York, 1956, p. 96.
15. *Beliefs of a United Methodist Christian*, p. 11. Italics mine.

16. Haste characterized the 1972 General Conference's vote on the Theological Commission's recommendation. According to one report, the matter was treated with only casual interest and the vote was taken after less than 15 minutes of discussion. See "The Problem of Pluralism," p. 36.

17. *Time,* January 7, 1985, p. 83.

18. Tom Wright, "Where Shall Doctrine Be Found?" in *Believing in the Church,* ed. John V. Taylor, Morehouse-Barlow Co. Inc., Wilton, CT, 1982, p. 139.

19. John Knox Press, Atlanta, 1981.

20. *Wesleyan Theological Journal,* vol. 15, no. 2, pp. 33-44. Culp is identified in the Journal as a faculty member at Olivet Nazarene College.

21. Culp, "Dialogue," p. 40.

Chapter 1

1. Steven V. Monsma, "Principled Pragmatism and Political Pluralism," *Christian Scholar's Review,* vol. 6, nos. 2 & 3, p. 157.

2. Monsma, p. 159.

3. Edwin H. Maynard, "Delegates Take Pluralism Seriously," *The Interpreter,* September 1984, p. 3.

4. Maynard, *The Interpreter,* p. 3.

5. Woodie W. White, "Inclusiveness is Working!", *Circuit Rider,* September 1984, p. 7.

6. Emerson Colaw, *Beliefs of a United Methodist Christian,* Nashville, Tidings, 1972, p. 8.

7. Richard G. Hutcheson, Jr., *Mainline Churches and the Evangelicals,* Atlanta, John Knox Press, 1981, p. 139. Cf. also p. 177. Colaw also makes use of this image, p. 9.

8. John Hick, "Pluralism and the Reality of the Transcendent," *The Christian Century,* January 21, 1981, p. 46. Hick teaches at the United Methodist related Claremont School of Theology.

9. John Wesley, *Works,* Grand Rapids, Baker Book House, 1979 (Reprint of the 1872 Edition), 7:47-48; 197-198; 353.

10. Hick, p. 48.

11. John Hick, "Jesus And the World Religions," *The Myth of God Incarnate,* ed. John Hick, London, SCM, 1977, p. 176.

12. *The Myth of God Incarnate,* p. 178. With regard to Hick's claim that the doctrine of incarnation is devoid of meaning, see Thomas V. Morris, *The Logic of God Incarnate,* Ithaca, Cornell University Press, 1986.

Chapter 2

1. James V. Heidinger II, "The Problem of Pluralism," *Good News*, May-June 1982, p. 37. Others who have pointed out similar confusion include Ira Gallaway, *Drifted Astray*, Nashville, Abingdon, 1983, pp. 53-61; and Paul Mickey, *Essentials of Wesleyan Theology*, Grand Rapids, Zondervan, 1980, pp. 22-23.
2. Roger Trigg, *Reason and Commitment*, Cambridge, Cambridge University Press, 1973, p. 153, 154.
3. Patrick Sherry, *Religion, Truth and Language Games*, New York, Barnes and Noble, 1977, p. 175. According to Sherry there is a tradition for these two senses of truth, going back to Plato.
4. T. F. Torrance, *Reality and Evangelical Theology*, Philadelphia, The Westminster Press, 1982, p. 66.
5. Perhaps it should be pointed out that philosophers often distinguish between sentences and statements. To cite Richard Swinburne: "Sentences are words strung together in conformity with the rules of grammar. . . . However, a meaningful sentence is to be distinguished from what it expresses. . . . Different sentences may make the same statement, and the same sentence on different occasions of its use may make different statements." *The Coherence of Theism*, Oxford, The Clarendon Press, 1977, pp. 11-12. If this distinction is recognized, it appears that the word "statement" in our definition of pluralism means "sentence."
6. John Courtney Murray, *The Problem of God*, New Haven, Yale University Press, 1964, pp. 45-46.
7. *Reason and Commitment*, pp. 34-35.
8. *Religion, Truth and Language Games*, p. 12 (citing the view of Paul van Buren).
9. William J. Abraham, *Divine Revelation and the Limits of Historical Criticism*, Oxford, Oxford University Press, 1982, p. 91. Abraham's entire volume is a very important work bearing on these issues. See especially Chapter 4, "Divine Action and Mythology," which includes a critique of Hick's interpretation of the Incarnation. To hold a factual understanding of the Christian tradition is not to assume that all theological language is of this type. As Abraham says, it would be "insensitive and unimaginative" to think all discourse about divine action is factual and explanatory (p. 90). The language of analogy, metaphor, etc. must obviously be taken into consideration in any full-blown account of theological language. It has not been my purpose to provide such a full-blown account, but only to highlight the basic difference between those who accept traditional creedal affirma-

tions as factual, and those who do not. Abraham has dealt elsewhere with the issue of divine action in modern Methodist theology. See "Inspiration, Revelation and Divine Action: A Study in Modern Methodist Theology," *Wesleyan Theological Journal,* Vol. 19, no. 2; "On How to Dismantle the Wesleyan Quadrilateral: A Study in the Thought of Albert C. Knudson," *Wesleyan Theological Journal,* vol. 20, no. 1.

10. Paul L. Holmer, *The Grammer of Faith,* San Francisco, Harper & Row, 1978, p. 12.

11. Basil Mitchell, "I Believe: We Believe," in *Believing in the Church,* ed. John Taylor, Wilton, Connecticut, Morehouse-Barlow Co., Inc. 1982, p. 15. *Emphasis* as in original. Much of the discussion in this book is relevant to the United Methodist Church.

12. I had finished writing this material before I discovered Geoffrey Wainwright's helpful discussion of "Creeds and Identity" in *Doxology,* New York, Oxford University Press, 1980, pp. 189-194. Some of our points are similar.

13. T. F. Torrance, *Space, Time, and Resurrection,* Grand Rapids, Eerdmans, 1976, p. 59.

14. Anthony Thiselton, "Knowledge, Myth, and Corporate Memory" in *Believing in the Church,* p. 64. *Emphasis* as in original.

15. *Believing in the Church,* p. 65. *Emphasis* as in original.

16. *Believing in the Church,* p. 66.

17. Thus it may be legitimate, as suggested above, to distinguish between doctrinal pluralism and theological pluralism; for legitimate theological pluralism must rest on essential doctrinal unity (cf. *Doxology,* p. 191). This is not to suggest, however, that in all cases we can draw simple and clearcut distinctions between doctrine and theology.

18. I do not mean to suggest that all liberation theology is rooted in classical orthodox theology. Much of it is not. But my point is that it can be, and when it is, there is no reason to doubt that it is a legitimate expression of Christian truth.

19. *Divine Revelation and the Limits of Historical Criticism,* p. 27. When I speak of God's intervention in the natural world, I do not mean to imply in deistic fashion that the natural order functions of its own accord. To the contrary, the natural order is continually sustained by the power of God. When God performs a miracle, He violates the regularity He normally maintains in the world for the purpose of revealing Himself in a special way.

20. As Wesley put it, "The Scriptures are the touchstone whereby Christians examine all real or supposed revelation." *The Letters of the Reverend John Wesley,* London, Epworth Press, 1931, II, p. 117. Cited by Allan Coppedge, "John Wesley and the Issue of Authority in Theological Pluralism," *Wesleyan Theological Journal,*

vol. 19, p. 71.
21. Stephen W. Sykes, *The Integrity of Anglicanism*, New York, Seabury, 1978, pp. 6-7.

Chapter 3
1. John Wesley, *Works*, Grand Rapids, Baker Book House, 1979 (reprint of the 1872 edition), 4:419. For Wesley's reference to the broad foundation of Methodism, see p. 469. In subsequent notes, where possible, I have also cited the parallel reference in the Abingdon Bicentennial Edition of *The Works of John Wesley*. The only volumes available at the time of this writing are the first two volumes of "Sermons," edited by Albert C. Outler. References to these volumes are in parentheses.
2. *Works*, 8:249.
3. Cf. *Works*, 9:56-57, 126-127; 10:347-348; 13:215-216.
4. *Works*, 3:211. The phrase occurs in a letter to John Newton, who is identified in the place cited only as "a friend."
5. *Works*, 5:485 (2:70).
6. For example, see his sermons on the nature and use of the law: *Works*, 5:433-466 (2:1-43). See also his sermon on "Free Grace" for a sharp critique of the Calvinistic view of the eternal decrees of God: 7:373-385.
7. *Works*, 5:78 (1:220-221).
8. *Works*, 6:276 (2:483).
9. John Wesley, *Explanatory Notes Upon the New Testament*, Salem, Ohio, Schmul Publishers, p. 560. Cf. also Wesley's note on I Corinthians 11:18.
10. *Works*, 6:328 (2:555).
11. *Works*, 6:328 (2:555). This passage also contains Wesley's defense of Pelagius. For his remarks on Servetus, see *Works*, 1:318; 6:201 (2:378); 10:350-351.
12. *Works*, 9:126.
13. *Works*, 9:127.
14. *Works*, 10:348.
15. *Works*, 3:377-378. Italics mine.
16. *Works*, 5:9 (1:121). Cf. pp. 60-61; 205 (1:194-195; 405). Rex D. Matthews has pointed out that the notion of faith as rational assent to propositional truth is most prominent in Wesley's early writings. However, throughout his career Wesley retained the notion that rational assent to propositional truth is an aspect of faith. See Matthews' essay "With the Eyes of Faith: Spiritual Experience and the Knowledge of God in the Theology of John Wesley," in *Wesleyan Theology Today*, ed. Theodore Runyon, Nashville, Kingswood Books, 1985, pp. 410-411.

17. *Works,* 6:205 (2:384).
18. *Works,* 6:205 (2:385).
19. *Works,* 5:503 (2:94).
20. *Works,* 5:493 (2:82).
21. *Works,* 5:494; 495 (2:83-84).
22. *Works,* 5:496 (2:85-86).
23. *Works,* 5:499 (2:89).
24. This raises a number of important epistemological issues about the relationship between will and belief. The question of what role the will has in belief has been, and still is, vigorously debated. Wesley recognized that some mistaken opinions may be willful, and therefore culpable. However, only God can judge when this is the case. See *Works* 5:495 (2:84).
25. *Works,* 5:502 (2:92-93).
26. *Works,* 5:502 (2:93).
27. *Works,* 5:497 (2:87). The phrase comes from Romans 9:5. See also Wesley's comment on this verse in his *Explanatory Notes Upon the New Testament.* There is disagreement over whether this particular verse actually affirms Christ's deity. It is unclear from a strictly grammatical standpoint, which is reflected in different translations. Compare, for example, the R.S.V. and N.I.V.
28. *Works,* 3:315. Cf. 6:351-352 (2:588).
29. *Works,* 8:340.
30. *John Wesley,* ed. Albert C. Outler, New York, Oxford University Press, 1964, pp. 492-493.
31. *Works,* 10:81-82.
32. *John Wesley,* p. 92. Outler makes this point in his Introduction to Wesley's sermon, "Catholic Spirit."
33. *Works,* 12:475.
34. See, for example, *Works,* 5:234-236 (1:449-452).

Chapter 4
1. Ira Gallaway, *Drifted Astray,* Nashville, Abingdon, 1983, pp. 55- 56.
2. Richard G. Hutcheson, Jr., *Mainline Churches and the Evangelicals,* Atlanta, John Knox, 1981, p. 136.
3. Richard Swinburne, *The Coherence of Theism,* Oxford, Clarendon Press, 1977, p. 19.
4. *The Coherence of Theism,* p. 14.
5. Strictly speaking, perhaps this is not a theological truth claim but only a truth claim about theology. However, I do not think this affects the argument.
6. George A. Lindbeck, *The Nature of Doctrine,* Philadelphia, Westminster, 1984, p. 74.

Chapter 5

1. Paul L. Holmer, *The Grammar of Faith*, San Francisco, Harper & Row, 1978, pp. 1, 3.
2. The phrase "Wesleyan Quadrilateral" does not appear in our Doctrinal Statement but it has been commonly used in the past few years to refer to the four sources and guidelines. Note, however, that reference is made to "the Wesleyan appeal to the fourfold norms of Scripture, tradition, experience, and reason" (p. 45).
3. See Allan Coppedge, "John Wesley and the Issue of Authority in Theological Pluralism," *Wesleyan Theological Journal*, Vol. 19, No. 2, pp. 62-76. It is noteworthy that Albert C. Outler, who invented the phrase "Wesleyan Quadrilateral" admits that he has sometimes regretted coining the phrase for contemporary use "since it has been so widely misconstrued." Outler intended the phrase to be understood as a metaphor rather than literally. See his essay "The Wesleyan Quadrilateral—In John Wesley," *Wesleyan Theological Journal*, Vol. 20, No. 1, pp. 11, 16.
4. William J. Abraham, in his essay "The Wesleyan Quadrilateral," has shown that this is true in Wesley. The essay appears in *Wesleyan Theology Today*, ed. Theodore Runyon, Nashville, Kingswood Books, an imprint of the United Methodist Publishing House, 1985, p.122. The papers in this volume were read at the Bicentennial Consultation on Wesleyan Theology, held at Emory University in August of 1983.
5. William J. Abraham has surveyed the current options in the debate about the rationality of religious belief in *An Introduction to the Philosophy of Religion*, Englewood Cliffs, N.J., Prentice-Hall, 1985, chapters 7-10.
6. "The Wesleyan Quadrilateral," p. 124. Abraham is expounding Wesley's views in this passage.
7. "The Wesleyan Quadrilateral," p. 124.
8. Questions about the whole concept of canon and its closure are very much alive at present. See James Barr, *Holy Scripture: Canon, Authority, Criticism*, Philadelphia, Westminster, 1983, pp. 49ff.
9. John Wesley, *Works*, Grand Rapids, Baker, 1979 (reprint of the 1872 edition), 5:127; 129; 133 (1:290; 293; 297). As in chapter three, references in parentheses are to the Abingdon Bicentennial Edition of *The Works of John Wesley*.
10. Rex D. Matthews, "Reason, Faith, and Experience in the Thought of John Wesley," unpublished paper presented to the Seventh Oxford Institute of Methodist Theological Studies at Keble College, Oxford, 1982, p. 34.

11. Rex D. Matthews, " 'With the Eyes of Faith': Spiritual Experience and the Knowledge of God in the Theology of John Wesley," in *Wesleyan Theology Today,* p. 412.

12. Matthews, "Reason, Faith, and Experience in the Thought of John Wesley," pp. 34-35.

13. See Lawrence W. Wood, "Wesley's Epistemology," *Wesleyan Theological Journal,* Vol. 10, pp. 55-56.

14. Bruce C. Birch, "Biblical Theology: Issues in Authority and Hermeneutics," in *Wesleyan Theology Today,* p. 130.

15. Edwin Lewis, "The Fatal Apostasy of the Modern Church," *Religion in Life,* Fall 1933, p. 488.

16. According to Thomas A. Langford, this was true of the period from about 1890-1940. See his "Constructive Theology in the Wesleyan Tradition," in *Wesleyan Theology Today,* p. 56.

17. John Hick, "Jesus and the World Religions," in *The Myth of God Incarnate,* ed. John Hick, London, SCM, 1977, p. 176.

18. *The Myth of God Incarnate,* p. 183.

19. For a helpful discussion of the term "accurate" as applied to Scripture, see Paul A. Mickey, *Essentials of Wesleyan Theology,* Grand Rapids, Zondervan, 1980, pp. 107-119. For a well-argued article maintaining that the burden of proof lies on those who challenge the authenticity of any given Gospel passage, see Stewart C. Goetz and Craig L. Blomberg, "The Burden of Proof," *Journal for the Study of the New Testament,* Vol. 11, pp. 39-63.

20. *The Myth of God Incarnate,* p. 170.

21. Richard Swinburne, however, has challenged the common assumption that we can draw a line between an interpretation of a religious experience and the actual object of the experience. See *The Existence of God,* Oxford, Clarendon Press, 1979, pp. 257-260.

22. For more on the notion of revelation as an achievement verb, see William J. Abraham, *Divine Revelation and the Limits of Historical Criticism,* Oxford, Oxford University Press, 1982, pp.11-12.

23. James Barr, "Revelation Through History in the Old Testament and in Modern Theology," *Interpretation,* Vol. 17, p. 201. As his title indicates, Barr is primarily concerned with the Old Testament, but he points out that his argument also applies to the New Testament.

24. See *Divine Revelation,* pp. 10-11; 14-15.

25. *Divine Revelation,* p. 25. Abraham also defends the importance of divine speaking in *The Divine Inspiration of Holy Scripture,* Oxford, Oxford University Press, 1981, chapter 4.

26. *Divine Inspiration,* p. 89.

27. It may be noted that my argument here is anticipated in my earlier comments on the creed in chapter 2.

28. *Works,* 6:354 (2:591-592).

29. *Works,* 6:355 (2:593).

30. *Works,* 6:204-206 (2:383-386).

31. Basil Mitchell, *The Justification of Religious Belief,* New York, Seabury Press, 1973, p. 148.

32. John Courtney Murray, *The Problem of God,* New Haven, Yale University Press, 1964, pp. 51-52.

33. Leroy T. Howe, "United Methodism in Search of Theology," *Perkins Journal,* Vol. 28, (Fall 1974), p. 14.

34. This change in the philosophical climate has become so well known that even *Time* magazine has reported it. See *Time,* April 7, 1980, pp. 65-68.

35. Probably the best known work in this regard is that of Thomas F. Torrance. See for example his *Space, Time and Incarnation,* Oxford, Oxford University Press, 1969; *Reality and Evangelical Theology,* Philadelphia, Westminster, 1982.

Chapter 6

1. Geoffrey Wainwright, *Doxology,* New York, Oxford University Press, 1980, p. 8.

2. Schubert M. Ogden, "Doctrinal Standards in the United Methodist Church," *Perkins Journal,* Vol. 28 (Fall 1974).

3. Ogden, p. 20.

4. Ogden, p. 21.

5. For the Restrictive Rules, see chapter 1, note 6.

6. Ogden, p. 22.

7. Ogden speaks of theology being free rather than of theologians being free. However, I do not think I have misrepresented him in saying that his argument requires theologians to be exempt from doctrinal standards. For theology has no life of its own, but only as it is produced and promulgated by theologians. Thus, theology can be free only if theologians are.

8. Robert E. Cushman, "Church Doctrinal Standards Today," *Religion in Life,* Vol. 44, (Winter 1975).

9. Cushman, p. 402.

10. Cushman, p. 404. A good example of how this principle is applied would be John Hick's view of the classical creeds. While they gave acceptable expression to the significance of Jesus in earlier times, they do not do so today, according to Hick.

11. Cushman, p. 408.

12. Cushman, p. 405.

13. John Courtney Murray, *The Problem of God,* New Haven, Yale University Press, 1964, p. 48.

14. *The Problem of God,* p. 49.

15. It is ironic that Albert Outler, in his introduction to the 1972 Statement, cited John Courtney Murray in connection with "the historical consciousness" which is now supposed to dominate the Christian understanding of doctrine and dogma. See Albert C. Outler, "Introduction of the Disciplinary Statement," *Wesleyan Theology: A Sourcebook*, ed. Thomas A. Langford, Durham, N.C., The Labyrinth Press, 1984, p. 276. It is clear that, for Murray, historical consciousness does not involve viewing the classic creeds as mere landmarks with no status of finality.

16. Cf. George A. Lindbeck, *The Nature of Doctrine*, Philadelphia, Westminster, 1984, pp. 92-93.

17. Paul L. Holmer, *The Grammar of Faith*, San Francisco, Harper & Row, 1978, p. 19. Lindbeck also compares doctrine to grammar. See *The Nature of Doctrine*, pp. 79 ff.

18. *The Grammar of Faith*, pp. 19-20; cf. also p. 12.

19. *The Grammar of Faith*, p. 12.

20. *Doxology*, p. 177.

21. A few years ago, Professor Donald Bloesch conducted a survey of United Methodist seminary professors concerning their beliefs about the Trinity and the person and work of Christ. The survey revealed that only about 30 percent held an orthodox view of the Trinity. Cited by James V. Heidinger II in "Good News' Concern with Theological Education in the United Methodist Church," Wilmore, Kentucky, p. 7.

22. H. F. Woodhouse has suggested that three verdicts may be passed on theological proposals: guilty, not guilty, or not proven. " 'Guilty' would mean that the position was seen as going beyond the legitimate limits of pluralism; 'not guilty' would recognize it as a legitimate interpretation, presentation or formulation; 'not proven' would leave the final decision in suspense: it would mean that we are not willing to adopt the position, and may never come to adopt it, but are not prepared to state categorically that it falls outside the acceptable limits." "The Limits of Pluralism," *Scottish Journal of Theology*, Vol. 34, p. 8.

23. Thomas C. Oden, *Agenda for Theology*, San Francisco, Harper & Row, 1979, p. 106.

24. "The Order For the Consecration of Bishops," in *The Book of Worship*, Nashville, United Methodist Publishing House, 1964, p. 55.

25. Tom Wright, "Doctrine Declared," in *Believing in The Church*, ed. John Taylor, Wilton, CT, Morehouse-Barlow, 1981, p. 140.

26. Cf. Richard G. Hutcheson, Jr., *Mainline Churches and the Evangelicals*, Atlanta, John Knox, 1981, pp. 113-115.

Epilogue

1. "A Call to the Spiritual and Holy Life," *Circuit Rider,* June, 1986, p. 8.
2. "Introduction of the Disciplinary Statement," *Wesleyan Theology: A Sourcebook,* ed. Thomas A. Langford, Durham, N.C., The Labyrinth Press, 1984, p. 274.
3. From the forword to George Carey, *A Tale of Two Churches: Can Protestants and Catholics Get Together?* Downers Grove, Illinois, Inter-Varsity Press, 1985.
4. *Methodism,* London, Epworth Press, 1976, p. 94.

Index of Names

140